VIOLENCE
AND
WOMEN

www.ChironPublications.com

Cover design and interior formatting by Nelly Murariu

Printed primarily in the United States of America

Herkulaneischer Meisters known work derived from an original by Timomaco (3rd century BC) / Public domain

ISBN 978-1-63051-832-5 paperback
ISBN 978-1-63051-833-2 hardcover
ISBN 978-1-63051-834-9 electronic
ISBN 978-1-63051-835-6 limited edition paperback

Library of Congress Cataloging-in-Publication Data

Names: Chapman, Anita S., author.

Title: Violence and women : exploring the Medea myth / Anita S. Chapman.

Description: Asheville, NC : Chiron Publications, [2020] | Includes bibliographical references. | Summary: "The archetypal story of Medea is a cautionary tale for our era. Jason and Medea's marriage, favored by the gods, represents an attempt at a union of opposites very far from each other. They represent the masculine and feminine principles, covering a wide range of psychological, sociological, and historical aspects. This synthesis fails. In the myth, as Euripides presents it, the failure is caused by Jason's regression and submission to the exclusivity of the patriarchal principle—the Old King. Medea, who not only represents the feminine but also the forces of Nature and Transformation, is profoundly incompatible with this regression. She reacts! She destroys and creates havoc. This is what the unconscious does when it is not heard or denied. In the end Medea is saved by the gods, the divine principles or psychic laws that regulate the laws of Nature and Transformation in the psyche. They support her to the bitter end"— Provided by publisher.

Identifiers: LCCN 2020027358 (print) | LCCN 2020027359 (ebook) | ISBN 9781630518325 (paperback) | ISBN 9781630518332 (hardcover) | ISBN 9781630518349 (ebook)

Subjects: LCSH: Violence in women. | Women—Psychology. | Medea, consort of Aegeus, King of Athens (Mythological character) | Euripides. Medea.

Classification: LCC HQ1206 .C4486 2020 (print) | LCC HQ1206 (ebook) | DDC 305.48/42--dc23

LC record available at https://lccn.loc.gov/2020027358

LC ebook record available at https://lccn.loc.gov/2020027359

VIOLENCE
AND
WOMEN

*Exploring the
Medea Myth*

ANITA S. CHAPMAN

Respect for oaths has gone
To the wind. Do you, I wonder, think that the old gods
No longer rule? Or that
New laws are now in force?

—Euripedes, *MEDEA*

DEDICATION

For Elizabeth Rüf and Benjamin Hunningher
In Loving Memory

CONTENTS

Preface   11

PART ONE   **13**
Introduction   15
The Medea Rage   17
The Myth of Medea   24
Euripides: *Medea*   30

PART TWO   **81**
Historical and Cultural Background   83
Euripides' Place in Greek Theatre in Fifth Century BC   90
The Truth of Medea for the Greeks   99
The Universality of Medea's Truth   108

PART THREE   **113**
Edith   115
Jason   122
Medea & Jason   126
The Poet and the Women   142
Concluding Remarks   145

Epilogue   153
Bibliography   155

PREFACE

This project—exploring the phenomenon of violent women—started with a woman distraught, an arrogant man, and a Greek tragedy. In the background, there was the U.S. invasion of a sovereign nation, and a mounting host of natural disasters—hurricanes, floods, and forest fires. I soon realized that I was not only dealing with the never-ending conflict between *feminine* and *masculine* principles, but also with the eternal archetypal dynamics of the principles of anger and revenge.

Some of this material I presented in lectures to students at the International Seminar for Analytical Psychology in Zurich. Their enthusiasm and helpful comments encouraged me to write this book. Clearly, my experiences with analysands influenced and motivated me as well. I am indebted to Mike L. and Carol Cole Czeczot for their steadfast editorial assistance, and also grateful to Pedro Kujawski and Barbara Hess Kovaz for their valuable insights and suggestions. I was fortunate to find the cover illustration at the New York Archive for Research in Archetypal Symbolism.

PART ONE

*The fiercest anger of
all, the most incurable,*

*Is that which rages in
the place of dearest love.*

—Euripides, *Medea*

INTRODUCTION

In 2002, when forest fires were raging near Denver, Colorado, forest ranger Terry Barton said she had started the fire accidentally while she was burning a letter from her estranged partner. Later she confessed that the fire wasn't an accident at all, that she had knowingly and deliberately set off the terrible conflagration which consumed more than 138,000 acres of forest land, destroyed homes and other property, and directly or indirectly killed six people. I thought, "Now there's an angry woman."

Reflecting about the pyrophoric forest ranger, I started noting a number of other dramatic, tragic and sensational incidents in the United States, where there was a man in the background and a woman out-of-control. Near where I live in North Carolina, Brenda Kay McCutcheon was charged with shooting her husband, a plastic surgeon, in their home. In Texas, Clara Harris ran over her cheating husband with her car until she killed him. Then there was Andrea Yates, also in Texas, who drowned her five small children in the family bathtub, one by one. The oldest was seven. In South Carolina, Susan Smith locked her two children in the family car and pushed it into a lake. There was also Francine Hughes of Michigan, who, while her abusive partner was sleeping, set fire to his bed. That story became a best-selling book and TV movie. Of course, the name Lorena Bobbitt, who severed a part of her husband's male anatomy, became fodder for myriad crude jokes. I became curious about the subject of violence and women. As a Jungian analyst in private practice who has worked with angry women over the years, I thought perhaps there was something I could find to say about a woman's impulse to destroy and to self-destruct.

The term "domestic violence" is most often used to label physical violence that is done to women, which is pandemic. Consider that in the period July 2017–June 2018, in North Carolina more than 112,400 women reported being victims of domestic violence. Are we surprised? Shocked? Within our culture, "men" do that. Men do violent things to women, and to children. They have pretty consistently done so throughout recorded history. To me, it's amazing, for example, to stop and think that it wasn't until 1993 when, *apropos* the very media-visible atrocities going on in the former Yugoslavia at the time, rape finally was declared a war crime by a United Nations resolution. Alas, in the country where October has been designated national Domestic Violence Awareness Month, several recent judicial nominees to the U.S. Appeals Court have publicly argued in opposition to the passing of the Violence Against Women Act, or supported rulings against it. A recent example is David Porter's 2018 confirmation to a seat on the U.S. Court of Appeals for the Third District; he praised the U.S. Supreme Court's ruling in United States v. Morrison, which struck down part of the Violence Against Women Act.

THE MEDEA RAGE

The purpose of this work—what I want to focus on here, is violent women. And about one in particular, named Medea, who, in Euripides' classic Greek drama, took revenge against her husband for remarrying by killing their two children. When, here and there, a woman behaves in wild and irrational ways, and she gets media attention, public reaction can stir up echoes of the Spanish Inquisition and medieval witch trials. There is something really shocking about a violent woman. It can be argued that in some parts of the United States, if you are a woman, it is even taboo to be angry. Often, a woman is not supposed to feel, much less show, the normal human emotions of displeasure and anger. We hear a lot about men's anger. We might react with caution, tiptoe around it. If it's an angry woman, though, it's got to be someone with a serious problem.

Jung has said that, "There are as many archetypes as there are typical situations in life."[1] In our analytic practices we may be regularly confronted with the typical situation of a woman who is dealing with powerful emotions around issues of separation and divorce after her husband has been unfaithful to her, sometimes many years after the fact. One of the things I want to do here is explore what is going on emotionally and psychologically when a woman

---

1   C.G. Jung, "The Concept of the Collective Unconscious," *The Archetypes and the Collective Unconscious*, CW 9i, par. 99.

who experiences rejection, betrayal, and abandonment by her husband or committed partner not only gets really angry, but also finds herself behaving in terrible, violent, and destructive ways, including self-destructive ways.

Some years ago, a married woman (early in the second half of life) appeared in my consulting room. She was a highly educated professional. I'll call her Edith. When Edith came to see me, she was extremely distraught. She had recently discovered that her husband of more than twenty years, a man for whom she had made many sacrifices, was having an affair. It was with someone she knew. Edith confessed that when she found out her husband was having sex with this woman, she flew at him like a fury and attacked him physically. She wanted to choke him to death. He was, of course, able to fight her off. Then, in his presence, she started smashing precious personal objects belonging to him. According to Edith, her husband just stood there watching her with an expressionless face. He shrugged his shoulders and told her she was crazy and needed to see a psychiatrist.

Then, when he was away from home, she ransacked his closets, went through the pockets of his suits, riffled through his desk drawers, opened his mail. She told me that her moods were swinging between homicidal and suicidal. Edith wasn't eating; she wasn't sleeping. She wasn't going to work either, because she couldn't keep herself from collapsing into spontaneous and uncontrollable weeping.

She was like one possessed. Feeling totally frustrated and really stuck, sitting across from me she cried out in a desperate voice, "Am I going crazy?" I shook my head. "No," I said. "That is the 'Medea rage.'"

What happened after I named the "Medea rage" was uncanny. Edith lowered her head and was silent for what seemed like a long time. As I sat with her, watching her, my fantasy was that she was slowly feeling her way down along the long line of development going right through her body, through her very being, layer by layer, to the archaic levels in the depths of her psyche which Jung calls the collective unconscious. It was as if, imaginatively, Edith was able to experience herself struggling against the grip of this overpowering, archetypal, dark Medea energy. By the time she looked up again, it was as if she had understood something, and she was calmer.

Jung, talking about the vital importance of myths, says, ". . . they explain to the bewildered human being what is going on in his unconscious and why he was held fast." The phenomena of the unconscious, according to Jung, can be regarded as more or less spontaneous manifestations of autonomous archetypes, which can mold the destinies of individuals by unconsciously influencing their thinking, feeling and behavior, even if this influence is not recognized until long afterwards.[2] He reminds us that ". . .

---

2 "The Dual Mother," *Symbols of Transformation: Two*, CW 5, par. 467.

there is any amount of literary and historical evidence to prove that in the case of these archetypes, we are dealing with the normal types of fantasy that occur practically everywhere and not with the monstrous products of insanity."[3] As in, "I'm so mad at you, I could kill you."

Edith was an intellectually gifted woman. She was a superwoman, a perfectionist with very high standards in all areas of her life, who identified uncritically with patriarchal values and developed an incredible ability to rationalize and relativize her feelings. She could always keep on top of things. We might say she lived in her head. We also might say she was pretty one-sided. When Edith learned of her husband's infidelity, to her great amazement and chagrin, she suddenly found herself totally at the mercy of a fiery eruption of powerful and conflicting emotions. This, on top of everything else, made her feel stupid and ashamed, which only added to her inner chaos and confusion, and to her terrible suffering. Jung has pointed out that the effect of the archetype is always "strongest . . . where consciousness is weakest and most restricted . . . "[4], and that "the greatest danger threatening us comes from the unpredictability of the psyche's reactions."[5] In Edith's case, suddenly her instinct overrode her reason. Without

---

3   "Archetypes of the Collective Unconscious," *The Archetypes and the Collective Unconscious*, CW, 9i, par. 83.
4   "Concerning the Archetypes and the Anima Concept," *The Archetypes and the Collective Unconscious*, CW, 9i, par. 137.
5   "Archetypes of the Collective Unconscious," CW 9i, par. 23.

thinking, she flew across the room and went for her husband's throat.

Gradually, Edith and I started to follow the unfolding of her dreams, and to explore her personal history—as well as the other side of the story. After a while, with greater consciousness, she could take more distance from her situation and, on a deeper level, better understand and come to grips with her frightening, uncontrollable, and violent response to the pain and outrage she was feeling after she learned of her husband's betrayal. The myth of Medea became the jumping-off place as well as a point of reference for Edith's long personal analysis and process of individuation.

Jung tells us that, "When a situation occurs which corresponds to a given archetype, that archetype becomes activated and a compulsiveness appears, which, like an instinctual drive, gains its way against all reason and will, or else produces a conflict of pathological dimensions, that is to say, a neurosis."[6]

Applying Jung's words: "When a situation occurs which corresponds to a given archetype (in this case the situation of a wife being betrayed by her husband), that archetype becomes activated (as in Medea's desire for revenge), and a compulsiveness appears, which like an instinctual drive, gains its way against all reason and will (a woman finds

---

6   "The Concept of the Collective Unconscious," CW 9i, par. 99.

herself behaving in violent and destructive ways), or else produces a conflict of pathological dimensions, that is to say, a neurosis (Edith feeling totally stuck)."

The psychological reality of "Medea rage" covers a broad archetypal field, which has an extensive spectrum. In the past thirty-odd years, I have worked with a variety of women who came to see me because they had discovered that their marriage partners (or partners in committed relationships) were deceiving them, or because—even years after their divorce or an infidelity—they found they still had issues with their abiding grief and disillusionment. In certain respects, Edith's story comes pretty close to Euripides' drama. Thank goodness every woman who discovers her mate is unfaithful does not get homicidal or suicidal—or pyrophoric, like the forest ranger in Colorado.

A woman who experiences some serious kind of betrayal, rejection, or abandonment by her husband or partner, including the effects of disease or disability, illness, and even death—psychological as well as physical death—does not necessarily react violently and destructively in an explicitly Medea mode and concretely destroy her possibilities for the future, as did Susan Smith and Andrea Yates, the two women who drowned their children and are now in confinement for life. A woman's experience of rejection and betrayal and abandonment can take many forms. At some point there is a lot of anger and suffering.

There is usually terrible self-doubt and loss of self-esteem. Generally, there are strong feelings of vengeance and a desire for reprisal.

A husband or committed partner can have different kinds of affairs. He might have an affair with another person, woman or man, or an affair with his work—or with his golf game, or with his family of origin—with his mother (or his wife's mother!), or with Jack Daniels, drugs, or with pornography on the Internet. It could be an affair with himself, which he acts out through different varieties of spousal abuse. It could be several of the above.

Different women will react in different ways to their disappointment, disillusionment and hurt, when they discover that the men they love aren't the men they thought they were. One woman may throw the best plates against the wall, but then she'll roll up her sleeves and renegotiate the marriage in no uncertain terms. Another will look away and pretend she hasn't noticed anything, hoping it will all blow over. (It often does, or has to.) Someone else, who does not have a strong ego, may blame herself for her inadequacies and turn her anger inward. In either of the latter cases, the women may suffer self-destruction—some form of depression, physical illness, alcohol or drug abuse, or sexual dysfunction.

There are other possibilities, as well. With a healthy self-esteem, one woman will immediately pack up her bags (and her children, if that applies) and depart; another will pack up his bags and throw her partner out the door. Of course, there is always the woman who will deal with these things in *ze French vay*, and take a lover of her own. Just how the "Medea rage" and the urge for revenge manifests itself will be affected by a woman's personal history, the phase of life she's in and, in general, on what gets constellated in her individual psyche. In Jung's words, "The archetype… takes its color from the individual consciousness in which it happens to appear."[7]

THE MYTH OF MEDEA

I would like to retell the old story of Medea and explore and interpret this mythologem, this mythological motif, in particular in the way the Greek playwright, Euripides, did in his famous tragedy of retaliation and violent revenge. With poetic license, Euripides used the ancient saga of Jason's betrayal of Medea not only to say something to an Athenian audience of the late fifth century BC about the way a man treated a woman long ago, but also to say something about what was happening on different levels in Greek society in the time during which he was writing. Interestingly, and we'll get back to this, Euripides' *Medea*

---

7   "Archetypes of the Collective Unconscious," CW, 9i, par. 6.

was composed in 431 BC, just one year before the outbreak of the 27-year-long Peloponnesian Wars, and the militarism that destroyed the political and cultural influence of Athens in the Mediterranean world.

Medea! The name comes from the Sanskrit concept of *medha*, or female wisdom. Connected with the feminine art of healing, the name Medea was also related to medicine.[8] In archaic times, because a woman could create life, she often had a magical significance. According to Erich Neumann, in her time Medea was considered to be a mana figure who represented the principle of transformation. "But in her the declining matriarchate is already devalued by the patriarchal principle…" The mythical reality she personified was reduced and negativized. Originally, Medea was considered a goddess but, in the patriarchally colored version of her myth, she became a witch.[9]

Over the centuries, Medea has gotten a pretty bad rap. She has been called a sorceress, a murderer, and a madwoman. In other words, she is usually looked upon as someone who was crazy or inherently evil. However, in Karl Kerenyi's opinion, Euripides is "the only poet in whom (she) finds a worthy portrayer."[10]

What I want to do first is give a close reading of Euripides' drama, suggest an interpretation and, to illustrate this

8   Barbara G. Walker, ed., *The Women's Encyclopedia of Myths and Secrets*, San Francisco: Harper and Row,1983, 628.

9   Erich Neumann, The Great Mother, 288.

10   See Carl Kerenyi, *Goddesses of Sun and Moon*, 25.

particular archetypal phenomenon of the vengeful violent woman, include some anecdotes and commentary about events and issues in the greater collective where we all live that reflect it. I hope I can shed some light on the source of what I refer to as the "Medea rage," this terrible impulse to destroy and/or *self*-destruct that some women experience when they discover they have been rejected, betrayed, and abandoned, or realize that they are being abused.

Certainly, women can experience these awful feelings of disappointment and envy and anger with same-sex partners, and with good friends, male or female, and there's that aspect of a man's *anima* that we know can feel and express the "Medea rage," but what I am mainly focusing on here is the suffering of a heterosexual married and/ or deeply committed woman when she discovers she has been betrayed by the man to whom she has given her love and trust.

I will suggest examples of how the Medea archetype looks on the street, not to trivialize it, but to demonstrate how unconscious archetypal forces live around us in human behavior and pain every day. With an eye to presenting issues that come up in analytical practice, I also hope Medea will help us to better understand why some of the women we work with are in fact unhappy, angry, and bitter about so much of their lives, and why it is rather more complicated than what I have heard some Jungian colleagues, with a wave of the hand, dismiss as an *animus* problem.

One of the major contributions of Jung's work has to do with the analysis and development of the relationship between the individual and the collective aspects of society and of civilization. On a deeper level, what I'll be exploring here, symbolically as well as concretely, is the phenomenon of the *masculine* violation of the *feminine* as it is portrayed in Euripides' version of the Medea myth, suggesting not only how this looks on a personal level, but also raising the question of its timeless and universal significance.

Who was Medea? To give a little background and refresh your memory, Medea was an Asian princess, the daughter of the king of Colchis, Aeëtes (whose name, in some stories, has been connected to that of Hades, the god of the underworld), and she was the granddaughter of the sun god, Helios. Her mother was called Idyia, or "she who knows." Medea was a priestess in the temple of Hecate, the goddess of the crossroads and the mother of all witchcraft and witches. Of Hecate, Kerenyi says, "(She) commands the secret knowledge that is not Apollonic; in her the lunar displays its understanding of the most secret exits and entries, of life's origin and its termination."[11] From an early age Medea learned from Hecate about special herbs and potions, about poisons and antidotes. Medea has quite a reputation, as we have said, as a goddess of transformation, and as a sorceress and a magician. Today we might

---

11   Ibid., 33.

also call her a professional, a woman who, like her mother, Idyia, knew about many things. Kerenyi refers to Medea as a scientist.

To refresh your memory of the myth, Jason, to reclaim his usurped patrimony, has to fetch the Golden Fleece for his evil uncle, Pelias. He gathers fifty semidivine men to build a ship, the Argo, and sails forth with them to the other side of the world on a hero's journey. After many adventures, the handsome stranger with his long blond hair flowing down his back arrived in Colchis with the Argonauts. When he asked King Aeëtes to support him on the final stage of his quest for the Golden Fleece, Medea— with her golden eyes covered in a silver veil—was quietly present. On the spot she fell passionately in love with Jason. The story goes that Hera, the patroness of Jason and the Argonauts and, as we know, also the patroness of marriage, persuaded Aphrodite to get Cupid to shoot his arrow deep into Medea's heart.[12]

The Old King of Colchis, Aeëtes, had no intention of helping this fascinating young man and his hearty band of young sailors, but rather saw them all dead. He gave Jason three impossible tasks: The hero had to plow a field with fire-breathing bulls, sow a dragon's teeth and fight the fierce warriors that sprang up from them and, finally, slay

---

12   For the story of Medea and Jason leading up to the events in Euripides' drama, I consulted Carl Kerenyi, *Goddesses of the Sun and Moon*, 20-40, and *The Heroes of the Greeks*, 247-278. Also Edith Hamilton, *Mythology*, 117-130.

the great serpent that was guarding the Golden Fleece. The dazzling Medea risked everything to do everything that was in her power to assist him. Yes! Jason fell for her as well. He swore eternal love and gratitude to this beautiful princess with the exotic eyes. Ultimately, it was she who was instrumental in Jason's successful achievement of his heroic quest, as Hera knew she would be. It was because of Medea's help that Jason was able to capture the Golden Fleece. With the symbol of authority and kingship in hand, his goal accomplished, he could return from his daring journey unharmed.

The story of Medea starts out very romantically. Leaving family and homeland, abandoning her father and killing her brother (we'll go back to that later), Medea eagerly followed Jason. After they fled Colchis, he married her, and eventually brought her safely back to Greece to live in Corinth, where they had two children. Alas, as we know, Medea and Jason did not live happily ever after. Ten years later, behind Medea's back, Jason married the Corinthian princess, Glauce. In Euripides' tragedy, to retaliate and get her revenge on the perfidious hero, Medea murders Glauce and her father, King Creon. Finally, and horribly, she kills her and Jason's two young sons.

EURIPIDES: *MEDEA*

And now to Euripides' tragedy. We need to keep in mind that Euripides' *Medea* was originally written for and watched by a late fifth century BC Athenian/Greek audience. His sources would have been Homer (ninth century BC poet), Hesiod (eighth century BC poet, *Theogony*), Pindar (early fifth century BC lyric poet, *Odes*), and Herodotus (early fifth century BC historian). Apparently, there is some speculation whether Euripides was the poet who introduced into the Medea mythologem the motif of child murderer. The translation of this play, which I am working from, is by the English theater historian and scholar, Philip Vellacott.[13]

First, I want to introduce just a few things about the mechanics of the theater in ancient Greece, which were decidedly unrealistic. There was a Chorus. In Euripides' time, the main actors as well as the members of the Chorus wore masks; to distinguish themselves, the main characters' masks were bigger than those of the Chorus. The large mouths of the masks are thought to have been used as megaphones. The main actors also padded their bodies and wore long flowing robes (chiton) and platformed boots (cothurne). They had to portray larger-than-life characters and, of course, they also had to be seen and heard from a

---

13   Euripides' *Medea and Other Plays*, 17–61. Page references to quotations from *Medea* have been omitted; with this edition of the play in hand, they are not difficult to find.

great distance, as the plays were performed outdoors in amphitheaters, usually in a beautiful setting where two hillsides came together and where there was a natural hollowed-out circular playing area at the bottom.[14]

Euripides' fifth century BC version of the ancient story of Medea takes place in Greece, in Corinth. The setting is the courtyard in front of Jason's and Medea's house. It is the wedding day of Jason and King Creon's daughter, Glauce. Medea has only heard about the wedding this morning.

The Exposition of the drama begins with a soliloquy spoken by the Nurse—the old woman, the slave, who attends Medea as her personal servant and confidant. Speaking *"to earth and heaven,"* the Nurse gives the background history of Medea, and she informs us about what is going on right this minute. She gives us very important information. We discover, for example, that even though Medea came to Corinth as an exile from a barbarian country, came as a foreigner, she has *"earned the citizens' welcome."* We also learn that, to Jason, Medea has been *"all obedience."* Expressing the collective values of her time, the Nurse says, *"in marriage that's the saving thing, when a wife accepts her husband's will."* So right from the beginning we

---

14   For all information in this study about the conventions of Classical Greek theater, and the Greek playwrights, I am indebted to Phyllis Hartnoll, *A Concise History of the Theatre*, 7-31, and Macgowan & Melnitz, *Golden Ages of the Theater*, 1-20.

know that Medea is not only respected by the community she lives in as Jason's wife, and as a foreigner, but also that she has accepted the fifth century BC Greek collective's idea of what a good wife is—which in some quarters actually still sounds pretty familiar.

We quickly learn, however, that on this day there has been a serious clash of conflicting expectations in this marriage. As a man of civilized Greek society, Jason, perhaps a bit too casually under the circumstances, assumes that his wife is going to submit to his will in all things, including his expedient marriage to a younger woman, who also happens to belong to the local royal family. Even though she comes from a *"barbarian country,"* Medea's hopes for her marriage are very different. When the play begins, she is desperate because her expectations have been completely dashed. We, the audience, can hear her lamenting in the background as we listen to what the Nurse is reporting on the foreground:

> *Scorned and shamed,*
> *She raves, invoking every vow and solemn pledge*
> *That Jason made her, and calls the gods as witnesses*
> *What thanks she has received for her fidelity.*
> *She will not eat; she lies collapsed in agony,*
> *Dissolving the long hours in tears.*

Remember my analysand, Edith? *"She will not eat; she lies collapsed in agony, / Dissolving the long hours in tears."*

Totally devastated, Medea is by no means acquiescing peaceably to the fact that another woman is going to take her place in Jason's and her house. Obedient as she has apparently been so far, fitting in, adapting herself to life in a different culture, as she says later, *"Let no one think me a weak one, feeble spirited / A stay at home."* In this instance she absolutely does not quietly accept her husband's will. She is being difficult. She is demonstrating that she has personal feelings about the matter and—however inconvenient it might be for Jason—that, as if he didn't know, she has a will of her own. Medea is a woman with a lot of temperament and a strong *ego.* As the Nurse reminds us, *"The mind of a queen / Is a thing to fear. A queen is used / To giving commands, not obeying them; / And her rage once roused is hard to appease."*

Knowing what Medea has gone through for him, and with him, and knowing her history and reputation, we may certainly ask ourselves, what was Jason thinking of when, behind Medea's back, he married a younger woman and planned to bring her home with him to their house. But according to Greek law in fifth century BC, marriage to a foreigner was not legally binding, and Jason was acting within the law when he took a Greek woman to wife.[15] But, we may ask as Euripides does in this play, did that make it right?

---

15   See Philip Vellacott's "Introduction" to *Medea,* 8.

In the Exposition of the drama, the next character to appear on the stage is the Tutor. He is accompanied by Medea and Jason's two young boys, Mermerus and Pheres. The Nurse lets the Tutor know exactly how she feels about Jason's marriage to King Creon's daughter. She tells him that *"an honest slave suffers in her own heart the blow that strikes her mistress. / It was too much, I couldn't bear it; I had to come / Out here and tell my mistress's wrongs to earth and heaven."* The Tutor, who is also a slave, brings more information, and worse news still. Apparently, while Jason is standing by and doing nothing to prevent it, Creon, who has heard all about Medea's rage and her impassioned threats against the royal family, is going to banish from Corinth not only his new son-in-law's first wife, but also their two sons. The clearly disillusioned Tutor says, *"Old love is ousted by new love. Jason's no friend to this house…. These boys are nothing to their father; he's in love."*

The exchange between the Nurse and the Tutor at the very beginning of the play is most significant because in this upstairs/downstairs household, as servants, these two characters are close to the lives of Medea and Jason. From the beginning, there is no question about whose side they are on. In fact, the Nurse says she has to keep herself from raining curses down on her master's head. She knows Medea well, and she is most apprehensive about what will happen when Medea learns she has been banished:

The dark cloud of her lamentations
Is just beginning. Soon, I know,
It will burst aflame as her anger rises.
Deep in passion and unrelenting,
What will she do now, stung with insult?

"What will she do now, stung with insult?" The Nurse fears that, in this dark and heavy atmosphere, lightning will strike. These lines bring to mind again the news story about Terry Barton, who, when her partner rejected her in a letter, deliberately set the forests around Denver ablaze. It also brings to mind the story about Clara Harris, the woman in Texas who, soon after catching her husband in bed with his girlfriend, ran over him with her car until he was quite dead. The Nurse is asking when and how will the dark cloud of Medea's lamentations burst into flame?

Already in the Exposition of Euripides' drama, we can start to identify some of the elements which combine to arouse serious feelings of anger in a woman, and the impulse to destroy, and/or self-destruct: Broken promises, disappointment, thwarted expectations, and humiliation.

At this point in the play, the Chorus of Corinthian Women enters, and the Rising Action of the tragedy begins. There were traditionally fifteen women in the Euripidean Chorus (that is, men wearing the masks of women). Its members speak individually, in small groups, and as a whole. They provide choral interludes separating the acts. They speak and chant and dance.

They comment on the conflict and the action of the play, and may embody different aspects of collective values, for example, what "people" are saying, what "everybody" thinks, what "we" should do. They can also represent the different voices in our own heads when we, as the audience, are in conflict over an issue being aired on the stage and are considering things this way and that way, and the other way. Sometimes the Chorus gives historical background, sometimes they philosophize. The Chorus can be highly opinionated, but it can also be deeply compassionate. Usually, ultimately, the Chorus strives for the golden mean (the ideal moderate position between two extremes). And if we look closely, we might find the poet's thoughts in among their reflections.

In *Medea*, the Chorus of Corinthian Women start out sounding like a group of sympathetic but rather conventional neighbors. Of course, they have heard Medea's ravings in the background. They tell the Nurse that in this time of suffering, they are loyal to *"the House of Jason."*

The Nurse, however, sets them straight; Jason's house no longer exists. She tells them, *"all that is finished. Jason is a prisoner in a princess's bed."* When the Chorus overhears Medea in the background wishing for her death, the Women voice their concern:

> *Do not pray that prayer, Medea!*
> *If your husband is won to a new love —*

The thing is common; why let it anger you?
Zeus will plead your cause.
Check this passionate grief over your husband
Which wastes you away.

The first reaction of the Chorus reflects collective values, rationalizations: "Men *do* these things; get over it," or "God will take care of you," or "Eat something." We could say that at this point it sounds like the Corinthian Women are expressing *animus* opinions, generalizations—what people say.

To me, the Corinthian Women, when they first enter the scene, also sound like a type of couples counselor (this has been reported to me several times) who, for example, instead of quietly receiving and containing the deep personal hurt of a woman after she has been rejected and betrayed, and is agonizing in her disillusionment and her heartache during a session, plays it down in front of the woman's husband, saying things like, "Why are you so angry?" "Don't be so angry." "What's the matter? Did your parents divorce?" Or something else irrelevant. Before you know it, the wife's *negative animus* sets in and, sitting in the office of the couples counselor in front of her husband, she starts to feel like there's something wrong with her because she's unhappy her husband is sleeping with another woman, and that it's really her fault she's so upset. And that's when she seriously begins to wonder if she is going crazy, if her feelings and fantasies are pathological.

We understand that they are archetypal, that she is experiencing the "Medea rage," and that it is to be expected. We understand that she is entitled to feel hurt and angry.

The Chorus pleads with the Nurse to bring her mistress out to meet with them. Finally, Medea herself appears. She has been described to us by the Nurse, and we know that she is not doing well. We have heard her voice lamenting and grieving in the background from inside the house; we have heard her curse her children, curse Jason and all his people, and threaten the royal family of Corinth as well. It's interesting that in a script with very few stage directions, when Medea appears there are stage directions which read, *She is not shaken with weeping, but cool and self-possessed.* Medea, after all, is the daughter of a king and of a knowing mother, and she is the golden-eyed granddaughter of the sun god, Helios. She is also the protege and priestess of Hecate, the goddess of the crossroads and the mother of all witches and witchcraft. Medea knows who she is. Unlike many women, Medea knows she is a goddess. Poised and present, with her *persona* in place, Medea addresses the Chorus: *"Women of Corinth,"* she says, *"I would not have you censure me, so I have come."*

Medea has a long monologue here. First, she tells her neighbors she realizes she has to talk to them. She recognizes that she needs their understanding and sympathy, that she needs allies. *"I accept my place,"* she says, *"but this blow that has fallen on me / Was not to be expected. It has crushed my heart. / Life has no pleasure left, dear friends. I want to die."*

Considering that we know what is going to happen in the story, we may not forget that Medea says at this point in the action of the play, *"I accept my place."* In spite of her strong emotions to the contrary, no matter how much she hates it, no matter how much she would like to kill Jason (and you must know the feeling: "I'm so mad at you I could kill you!"), at this point Medea still accepts her place in Greek society, even though it is quite obvious to everybody that she does not like it one bit. As she seeks their sympathy and cooperation, she also says something to the Corinthian Women that ironically is perhaps a key to the nucleus of the "Medea" problem, and that of Medea and Jason. She says, *"Jason was my whole life; he knows that well. Now he / Has proved himself the most contemptible of men."* As Jung has pointed out, "The unpleasant side of… partnership is the disquieting dependence upon a personality that never can be seen in its entirety, and is therefore not altogether credible or dependable."[16]

Further along in her monologue to the Chorus, Medea has lines which go to the very depths of the seeds and roots of Western Culture, and which, even in modern

16   "Marriage as a Psychological Relationship," *The Development of Personality*, CW, 17, par. 332.

times, in certain parts of a country or demographic, or in certain elements of a population, die hard. For example, she says, *"For women, divorce is not / Respectable; to repel the man, not possible."* How Afghanistanian, we could say. How Victorian! Let's not forget that in the United States of America, the great modern experiment in democracy, until late in the 19th century, women were legally considered to be their husbands' property. They received the right to vote - by one vote - in 1920. These things that we take for granted today are in fact very recent historical developments, even in the Western world. The Equal Rights Amendment to the U.S. Constitution, proposed in 1923, finally received the necessary approval by 38 states on January 27, 2020, but because of other obstacles, ratification remains pending.

For sure, Medea is looking for sympathy from the Chorus, but also mutual understanding, when she continues:

> *If a man grows tired*
> *Of the company at home, he can go out, and find*
> *A cure for tediousness. We wives are forced to look*
> *To one man only. And, they tell us, we at home*
> *Live free from danger, they go out to battle: fools!*
> *I'd rather stand three times in the front line than bear*
> *   one child.*

Euripides has Medea telling it like it is in fifth century BC Athens. Historian J.M. Roberts, talking about Greek civilization at that time, says the following:

"Women... were excluded from citizenship... In Athens, for example, they could neither inherit nor own property, though both were possible in Sparta. Nor could they in Athens undertake a business transaction if more than the value of a bushel of grain was involved. Divorce at the suit of the wife was, it is true, available to Athenian women, but it seems to have been rare and was probably practically harder to obtain than it was for men, who seem to have been able to get rid of wives fairly easily. Literary evidence suggests that the life of most wives except those of rich men was the life of a drudge. The social assumptions that governed all women's behavior were very restrictive; even women of the upper classes stayed at home in seclusion for most of the time. If they ventured out, they had to be accompanied; to be seen at a banquet put their respectability in question. Entertainers and courtesans were the only women who could enjoy a certain celebrity, but a respectable woman could not. Significantly, in classical Greece girls were thought unworthy of education."[17]

---

17   J.M. Roberts. *The Hutchinson History of the World*, 227-228.

He adds, "Such attitudes suggest the primitive atmo-sphere of the society out of which they grew . . ." And this was the Golden Age!

Medea's words, *"If a man grows tired / Of the company at home, he can go out, and find / A cure for tediousness. We wives are forced to look / To one man only,"* make me think again of Andrea Yates, that bright girl who became an obedient wife, churchgoer, and a mother who kept having babies—even against doctor's orders. Whatever her psychopathology, it appears that this young woman was shackled to institutions—the church, the family, as well as to her husband, long before she was committed to a state prison and later to a mental hospital. We can imagine that, overwhelmed by the demands of her life—pregnancy and childbirth, again and again—with no help and no hope for a sense of personal autonomy—and feeling trapped, one by one Andrea Yates drowned her five small children in the bathtub. Out of the depths of her despair, she destroyed her future. As Jung has said, alluding to the monstrous products of insanity, "The pathological element does not lie in the existence of these ideas (I'd like to kill you), but in the dissociation of consciousness that can no longer control the unconscious."[18]

We keep hearing about shifts and changes in attitudes. Sometimes I wonder. In my practice, a young man of 29,

---

18   "Archetypes of the Collective Unconscious," CW 9i, par. 83.

apropos of something that was going on with him and his girlfriend, quite confidently assured me that there would always be a double standard. He was taught by his father to love them and leave them. As Medea put it, "If a man grows tired of the company at home, he can go out…"

Medea's words, and the story of Andrea Yates, and the remarks of this young man, all bring to mind the case of another analysand, a 38-year-old married woman, whose presenting issue was that she felt trapped in her marriage, as if she were drowning. She had a dream in which there was an image of a pacing leopard chained up on a small narrow balcony that jutted out from an apartment in a high-rise building. The leopard is an animal of Dionysus, the god of Earth, joy, and passion. In another dream, this woman was at the beach, struggling to keep her head above water, while her husband was trying to push her under. Fortunately, she was eventually able to develop a healthier and more conscious relationship with her heavy-handed concrete husband, as well as with the heavy-handed negative inner husband/*animus* that he embodied in her dream. In time, she was able to free some of that instinctive leopard energy within her and develop more personal autonomy in the greater context of her life.

Medea, continuing her opening monologue, continuing to try to establish a sympathetic rapport with the Corinthian Women, reminds the Chorus of her foreignness. For Medea, her foreignness is a real sore spot. We might call it a *complex*. Even with her strong ego and her impressive lineage, as someone who has come from a different place and is different on so many levels, she knows that, even though she is the daughter of a king and the granddaughter of a god, without the protection of a man she is vulnerable in Greek society, where foreigners had the same legal status as slaves. Everything she says at this point is psychologically and emotionally true. She is a mature adult. She cannot go back to her parents' house. She did what a woman is expected to do when she gets married, in those days as well as in our own day. She separated from her family of origin, and with her husband created a new family.

Medea is criticized by her detractors because she abandoned her father and killed her brother. Well, psychologically, a woman leaves her father when she marries. And she has to symbolically kill her brother when she gets married to deactivate the kinship libido that could lead to (psychological) incest.[19] Medea willingly gave herself to her husband, Jason, and to his life. And she fought for his life, and we know she really did kill for him. She murdered the Old King, Pelias, who had destroyed Jason's father and stolen his patrimony. (More about these things on a psychological level later.) Medea is telling the Chorus that now there is no place for her to turn—except herself.

19   See Erich Neumann, *The Origins and History of Consciousness*, 202-203.

There is no going back; she is stuck where she is. In *"the House of Jason,"* a younger woman will be sitting at the table in her former place.

Does Medea seem to be exaggerating her situation a bit when she says to the Women of Corinth, *"I was taken as plunder from a land at the earth's edge"*? We know, and the Chorus must know, that Medea ran after Jason. She really wanted him; she went with him willingly. Suffering the pain of rejection and betrayal, however, what she is saying here is that she feels as if she might just as well have been taken as plunder, rather than as what she had apparently mistakenly believed all along was the case—that she was being embraced by the man she married as a true love and as an equal.

Suffering the shock of Jason's sudden behind-her-back marriage to Princess Glauce, Medea feels, as some women have felt after her, that she was married as a means to an end, as a function, a convenience—to furnish a man's home, provide safe sex, create a family, and give respectability—but not because she was loved for herself, much less as an equal partner. Perhaps it is this disillusionment which often lies at the heart of the "Medea rage"—the woman's realization that she is not loved and cherished simply for being herself.

At the end of her monologue, Medea asks the Corinthian Women to please *"Say nothing,"* if she can *"find a way to work revenge on Jason for his wrongs to (her)."* She says, *"A woman's weak and timid in most matters; / The noise of war, the look of steel, makes her a coward. But touch her right in marriage, and there's no bloodier spirit."* We may not forget that Medea is also a protege of Hera, the goddess of marriage. And isn't it ironic that Hera was the patroness of Jason and the Argonauts?

Deftly stating her case to the Corinthian Women, by the end of her monologue, Medea has gained their compassion. They agree with her that *"To punish Jason will be just."* Finally, the Chorus says to her, *"I do not wonder that you take such wrongs to heart."*

By this critical juncture of the Rising Action of the drama, we know that Medea is having suicidal as well as homicidal thoughts, and also that she is thinking of ways to get back at Jason for his rejection and betrayal. We have heard the positions of the Nurse and the Tutor, Medea's household servants, and of her neighbors, the Corinthian Women. The people of Medea's household, as well as of her community, give to her and not to Jason their loyalty on this difficult wedding day.

Disappointment, broken promises and thwarted expectations, insult and humiliation, and the feeling of being trapped are all elements that can combine to incite in a woman feelings of anger and the impulse to destroy.

King Creon of Corinth next enters the scene! He wastes no time. While the Chorus is standing there listening, he tells Medea what we, the audience, already know—the bad news that the Tutor brought in earlier to the Nurse. Clearly, Creon is afraid of Medea and of what she might do. Thus (and obviously with Jason's tacit approval) he has unequivocally banished Medea and her two children from Corinth.

We can imagine another motive for Creon's decision to banish Medea and Jason's sons: Bloodline. He wants to be sure that his daughter Glauce's future offspring are going to become their father's undisputed heirs. We can also imagine why Jason is just standing by and accepting the fact that the king is banishing his first wife and their children. Life will certainly be a lot easier for him with Glauce, if Medea isn't around.

Now, we have heard from the Nurse that Medea is not only looking coldly on her children, but that in her ravings she has threatened Princess Glauce and Creon. With our own ears we have heard in the background Medea's wild talk—bemoaning her lot, cursing her children and Jason and all his people, and wishing she was dead. Onstage we have heard her say to the Chorus, however nicely, that she is looking for a way to revenge Jason. With Creon's pronouncement of her banishment, the plot definitely thickens. Medea realizes with horror that Jason is not only no longer her beloved and faithful husband, but that he also no longer embodies safety and protection for her and their children.

Historian Thomas Cahill, discussing male sexuality in fifth century BC Greece, tells us that "Any male citizen could do whatever he liked to anyone else, male or female, adult or child, so long as his object was not another citizen or a properly married woman. If a woman were divorced, as Medea was about to be, she was as fair game as anyone."[20]

Creon's decree of banishment and Jason's clear indifference to this decision propel Medea into the whirlwind of her worst *complex*. Wild and crazy talk that comes from disillusionment and anger and pain, starts to turn into concrete resolve. Now, indeed totally abandoned and without protection, Medea, the foreigner, really is an exile with nowhere to go.

This is Jason's ultimate rejection and betrayal. After what she did for him and went through for his sake because she loved him, he is standing by, doing nothing, as she totally loses her status in Corinth and, with their two boys, is being compelled to live a life of exile and impoverishment. This is indeed the ultimate treachery. Medea's back is to the wall. Her threats and curses are no longer academic.

Broken promises and thwarted expectations, insult and humiliation, the feeling of being trapped, and, on top of all that, estrangement and exile, poverty and

20   Thomas Cahill, *Sailing the Wine Dark Sea*, 134.

dependency—these are the elements that can combine to excite in a woman anger, as well as the determination to destroy.

Creon is quite frank when he says to Medea that her jealousy and resentment of his daughter, Glauce, cause him to fear her, for he knows that she is *"…a clever woman, skilled in many evil arts."* Medea answers bitterly, *"My reputation, yet again! A man of any shrewdness / Should never have his children taught to use their brains / More than their fellows."* As we know, Medea is highly educated. She is a specialist; Kerenyi calls her a scientist. Different from a lot of women of her time, her foreignness has many levels.

This exchange between Creon and Medea reminds me of something my analysand, Edith, told me. When she graduated with the highest academic honors from her professional training, her father, who had always set the highest standards for her, said after the commencement exercises, "I hate women like you."

I am reminded of another analysand who told me that when she got her M.S.W., her father quipped that, if he had known when she was a baby that she would grow up to be a social worker, he would have drowned her. These remarks were not taken to be funny. It has not been unusual for gifted women to report that they have felt they had to make themselves appear smaller and dumber so others would feel more comfortable around them. As Medea says of being a woman, *"if people rank / You above them, that is a thing they will not stand."*

Medea is indeed extremely clever, and, at this point in Euripides' drama, she is really thinking fast. Like many slaves and oppressed peoples, and like many women who are pushed into an inferior position against their will, she knows what someone wants to hear, and she knows how to say it to gain an advantage.

Incredibly, the Old King, in spite of everything he says he is aware of about Medea, is persuaded by her seemingly humble pleading to let her have one more day to manage her affairs and get her children ready for their exile from Corinth. Creon says, *"I'm no tyrant by nature. My soft heart has often / Betrayed me; and I know it's foolish of me now; / Yet nonetheless, Medea, you shall have what you ask... You can hardly in one day accomplish what I am afraid of."*

And he says he knows about Medea! He has just told her that he is afraid of her and of what she might do, and accused her of having skills in evil arts. This is an awesome example of how *ego* can get in the way of instinct. After all, the Chorus are listening. We can imagine that this king doesn't want the people to think he's a tyrant!

As soon as Creon leaves the scene, the Corinthian Women sympathize with Medea, visualizing the dread and danger of her miserable destiny as a wanderer. *"The grace of sworn oaths is gone,"* says the Chorus. *"Honour remains no more / In the wide Greek world, but is flown to the sky."*

Medea, meanwhile, is already starting to figure out how she can turn homicidal fantasy into terrible fact. It is as if the forces of revenge and retaliation are taking possession of her as we watch. Although she does not yet know exactly what she is going to do, Medea does know that on this one day she will strike three of her enemies—not only Jason, but Princess Glauce and King Creon as well. She considers different ways of retaliating against the king and the princess: *"The best way is the direct way,"* she says, *"which most suits my bent; / To kill by poison."* Now she is serious:

> *I'll wait a little.*
> *If some strong tower of help appears, I'll carry out*
> *This murder cunningly and quietly. But if fate*
> *Banishes me without resource, I will myself*
> *Take sword in hand, harden my heart to the uttermost,*
> *And kill them both, even if I am to die for it.*

It is important to remember that Medea's central hearth is dedicated to Hecate. When Jason insults Medea, he is offending Queen Hecate as well. Medea invokes the goddess who is her patroness: *". . . no one of them / Shall hurt me and not suffer for it!"* She prays, *"Let me work: / In bitterness and pain they shall repent this marriage, / Repent their houses joined, repent my banishment."*

We describe the archetypes as patterns of instinctive behavior, as pure, unvitiated nature. We talk about the killer instinct. Out of all the boiling emotions in the heart of Medea, the instinct to kill has now fully emerged; it has come seriously into relief. Remember my analysand Edith, who flew at her husband like a fury and, if in that moment, if she could have, she would have choked him to death. For Medea, the expression, "I'm so mad at you, I could kill you," is no longer metaphoric, hypothetical, hyperbolical, or academic. We know that Medea has killed for Jason. Now, after Jason's obvious complicity in Creon's pronouncement of her banishment, she is capable of killing him.

It is at this intense moment of the Rising Action of the play that the compelling and chilling climactic encounter between Medea and Jason takes place. The two conflicting forces meet. They collide.

Jason strides in talking. He is on the defensive, self-righteously blaming Medea for what is going to happen to her. Coming from his position of male entitlement and greater physical strength, not unlike an abusive husband dealing with his battered wife, he knows what is right and, if she doesn't agree with him, or isn't willing to go along with him in every way, she is crazy. In any case, Jason feels there is definitely something seriously wrong with her. In dysfunctional families, parents speak to their children this way. The leader of a country treats his citizens like this when he says that, if they disagree with his policies, they are being unpatriotic and disloyal.

In no uncertain terms, Jason tells Medea that it is her own fault she is being banished. *"You could have stayed in*

Corinth, still lived in this house. / If you had quietly accepted the decisions / Of those in power. Instead, you talked like a fool . . ." In other words, there's something wrong with you, Medea. You got angry. You brought this all on yourself. You're the bad person.

Can you imagine how the young, naïve, and romantic Princess Diana (who never even finished high school!) must have felt after her fairy tale wedding, when Prince Charles let her know that it was in fact Camilla Parker Bowles who was his queen of hearts? Eventually, to the great embarrassment of the British royal family, Diana did not quietly accept the decisions of those in power. She acted out. She behaved inappropriately. She upset the *status quo.* In Jason's words to Medea, she did *". . . not give up (her) ridiculous tirades against / The royal family . . ."* And that, we could say, led to Diana's ultimate undoing.

Continuing in his very patronizing tones, Jason says, *"Well, your angry words don't upset me . . ."* He tells Medea that he has *". . . carefully considered (her) problem,"* and that in spite of everything, he is going to give her and the boys some cash for the road. He could never bear ill will towards her.

"You filthy coward!" is Medea's unequivocal reply. *". . . if I knew any worse name / For such unmanliness, I'd use it . . ."* Medea confronts Jason fully. In detail she enumerates all the things she gladly did for love of him, all the things which helped him get to where he is today: *". . . I . . . lit the torch of your success."*

And in return for this you have the wickedness
To turn me out, to get yourself another wife,
Even after I had borne you sons! If you had still
Been childless I could have pardoned you for hankering
After this new marriage. But respect for oaths has gone
To the wind. Do you, I wonder, think that the old gods
No longer rule? Or that new laws are now in force?
You must know that you are guilty of perjury to me.
My poor right hand, which you so often clasped!
My knees
Which you then clung to! How we are besmirched and
mocked
By this man's broken vows, and all our hopes deceived!

Vividly, Medea portrays her fate as an exile to the man who, in fact, is forcing on her and their children not only poverty of wealth (which we know aggravates terrorism), but even more cruelly and dangerously, the poverty of dignity:

A marvelous
Husband I have, and faithful too, in the name of pity;
When I'm banished, thrown out of the country without
a friend,
Alone with my forlorn waifs.
Yes, a shining shame
It will be to you, the new-made bridegroom, that your
own sons,
And I who saved your life, are begging beside the road!

Coldly and cynically, Jason answers Medea. First, he accuses her of abusing him. Then he tells her that, as far as he is concerned, the credit for his and the Argonauts' *"…successful voyage was solely due / To Aphrodite, no one else divine or human."* Remember, the patroness of Jason and the Argonauts was the goddess of marriage, Hera, who, at the outset, enlisted Aphrodite's backing for this coupling. In effect, Jason denies not only the validity but also the significance of Medea's love for him. In his paternalistic and patronizing tones, he says, *"I admit you have intelligence… and I will not stress the point. Your services, so far as they went, were well enough …"*

This reminds me of another analysand who was still reverberating with "Medea rage" many years after her divorce. When she married a medical student, she was working full time to help him out and to support them both through his internship and residency, only to painfully discover after he got his M.D. that she was being displaced by a nurse he knew from the hospital. As Jason put it, *"Your services, so far as they went, were well enough …"*

Lest we lose sight of them, perhaps this is the place to review again and enumerate more specifically Medea's services to Jason. King Aeëtes, Medea's father, told Jason that before he could have the Golden Fleece, he had to perform three tasks. The young hero first had to plow a field with fire-breathing bulls. He then had to plant a dragon's teeth in the furrows. When armed warriors burst forth out of the ground, Jason had to fight them. Finally, he had to kill the immense serpent that was coiled around the tree where the Golden Fleece was hanging. Medea gave the man she was in love with a magic ointment to rub all over him and his weapons, so his body would be safe and his weapons invincible when he subdued the bulls and sowed the dragon's teeth. Then she instructed Jason to throw a rock in the midst of the dragon-teeth warriors so they would turn against each other and fight among themselves until they were all dead. Next, Medea lulled the terrible serpent that was guarding the Golden Fleece to sleep by singing to it, and Jason could just walk right by it and pick up the object of his heroic quest without any trouble. Because of Medea's help, no drop of Jason's or of the Argonauts' blood was shed in Colchis.

So that the heroic adventurers all got away safely, Medea abandoned her father and killed her brother. She made Crete safe for the Argonauts to have a rest on their trip back to Greece. Finally, to avenge the deaths of Jason's parents for him, she did use her dark arts to trick the murderer Pelias's own daughters to kill him by dismemberment. (More about the motif of dismemberment later.) Medea did a lot for Jason. She helped him to be the hero he was acclaimed to be and for which he took the credit.

Back to the play. Jason continues his response to Medea's confrontation. The way he sees it, she has gotten far more out of the deal than he has. It was because of him, after all, that she was delivered from *"a barbarous land."*

It was because of him she could reside in Hellas, a civilized country. His words drip with condescension, and irony: *". . . here you have known justice; you have lived / In a society where force yields place to law."* Clearly, Jason has not paid much attention to the law of the heart, or the law of human decency. Nor does he acknowledge the unseen, impersonal natural forces of life. He further points out to Medea that, if it hadn't been for him, *". . . if (she) still lived at the ends of the earth"* nobody would know who she was. Again ironically, he says, *"here your gifts are widely recognized, / You are famous . . ."* In other words, it is Medea's ingratitude to him which has caused her and their children to be forced into exile. Jason's sophistry, the way he manipulates language, is incredible.

Jason rationalizes away all argument. He totally disregards Medea's feelings—her crushed heart. With apparently no grasp of cause and effect, Jason embodies the principle of self-interest. He does not accept responsibility for his actions. He no longer accepts responsibility for Medea, or for his two sons by her. Evil is described as the absence of empathy. Euripides has Jason speak with the casual arrogance that creates terrorists. In the earlier words of the Chorus, Medea has indeed become *"An exile with no redress."*

Jason keeps talking defensively. To further justify himself and his actions, he says to Medea that wedding Princess Glauce was in her interest and in the best interest of their two children. His sophism is mind-boggling. He tells her that he married into the royal family because he wanted to solidify their economic security and social status. *"You need no more children, do you?"* he asks. *"While I thought it worthwhile to ensure advantages / For those I have, by means of those I hope to have."*

As far as we are aware, Medea is not barren. Do we know for sure that she did not want any more children from Jason? Had they talked about it? Jason's attitude could be described as the epitome of narcissism. He is telling her that she doesn't need any more children, but that it's all right for him to have more children from another woman. Is he implying that their sexual relationship is over?

As we look at the greater archetypal cloth of the Medea myth and all its diversity, for me, in the story of the famous opera diva Maria Callas, we can almost hear the reverberation of the story of Medea. Maria Callas seriously compromised her illustrious singing career to be with her lover, Aristotle Onassis, who apparently somewhat disparagingly called her his "canary." It is rumored that, when she became pregnant and was deeply happy to carry his child, he forced her to have an abortion before he left her to marry Jacqueline Kennedy.

Linda Schierse Leonard, in her book, *Meeting the Madwoman*, reminds us in the chapter called "The Rejected Lover" that not only was Maria Callas famous for her role as "Medea" in Cherubini's late 18th-century opera, but also that Pier Paolo Pasolini persuaded Callas to perform the title role in his provocative 1970s film, *Medea*.[21] Alas, in real life, in spite of the incredible opportunities she had to transform and redeem her suffering through her creative gifts, Maria Callas turned her profoundly personal disillusionment, grief, and anger in on herself and self-destructed. Deeply and seriously depressed, she became addicted to tranquilizers and sleeping pills as well as other medications. That was her response to her experience with a man who was the whole world to her and who crushed her heart. She killed her psychological children, her possibilities for the future, with opiates.

Meanwhile, back to Euripides. I would like to quote in full, eight lines of Jason's rationalizations:

> *Was such a plan, then, wicked?*
> (That he wanted to solidify their economic security and social status by marrying Glauce.)
> *Even you would approve*
> *If you could govern your sex jealousy. But you women*
> *Have reached a state where, if all's well with your sex life,*
> *You've everything you wish for; but when that goes wrong,*
> *At once all that is best and noblest turns to gall.*
> *If only children could be got some other way*
> *Without the female sex! If women didn't exist,*
> *Human life would be rid of all its miseries.*

---

21   See Leonard, 143-155. See also Terrence McNally, *The Master Class*, New York: Dramatists Play Services, Inc., 1996.

"If only children could be got some other way, / Without the female sex! If women didn't exist / Human life would be rid of all its miseries." In the voice of Euripides' Jason, do we hear the strain of misogyny traveling from the foundations of Western Civilization, through the Judeo-Christian tradition, right to the present day? And with test-tube babies becoming an option, and the possibility of human cloning in the offing, who knows? Given the medical and technological advances of our day, we now take for granted frozen embryos and sperm banks. I am told that there is even such a thing as mail-order artificial insemination. If children are no longer born out of loving relationships, if human reproduction can become deper-sonalized by modern technology, perhaps human life will finally be rid of all its miseries.

After Jason's tirade, the Chorus, which has been lis-tening, offers its opinion: *"Jason, you have set forth your case very plausibly. / But to my mind—though you may be surprised at this—/ You are acting wrongly in thus abandoning your wife."* In Euripides' drama, public opinion stays on the side of Medea.

At this point, Medea knows that her best answer to Jason is no answer. However, cutting to the quick, she does say, *"One word will throw you: if you were honest, you ought first / To have won me over, not got married behind my back."*

Untouched, unmoved, and firmly believing himself to be completely in the right—perhaps too firmly—Jason freely admits that the reason why he didn't discuss his plan to marry King Creon's daughter with Medea was because he knew she wouldn't agree to it. He continues to insist that the only reason he married Glauce was to *". . . give his children brothers / Of royal blood, and build security for (them) all,"* forgetting that Medea, however *"barbarian,"* was not only royal but semidivine. Jason never quite mentions his raw opportunism, or his sexual desire for the young and manipulable daughter of Creon, much less his lust for power. We, the audience, however, have already heard the candid comments and opinions of the Nurse and the Tutor, and the Women of Corinth, about all these things.

As if it is quite clear and simple, Jason tells Medea that she is a foolish woman who only has herself to blame for her exile because she *"called down wicked curses on the King and his house."* ("I'm so mad I could kill you all.") Jason has no feeling for Medea's disillusionment, her pain, her tormented pride. In effect, he is saying, "Don't be so angry, Medea. *Why* are you so angry? Look where your anger has gotten you! It's all your fault."

Continuing with his intellectualized alibis, Jason cavalierly repeats his offer to give Medea and their children financial assistance, as well as letters of introduction for the road. For Medea this is the penultimate insult. *"Go!"* she cries. *"You have spent / Too long out here. You are consumed with craving for / Your newly-won bride. Go, enjoy her!"* Behaving as if he has really done his best to help his first wife and their two sons as they are about to go into miserable exile, and that it is now really Medea's problem, with his head held high, Jason exits from the climactic scene of confrontation between him and his Asian wife.

By this time, Medea's deep disappointment, her rage and grief have turned into feelings of unutterable revulsion and contempt for the man who was once her beloved hero. In the words of the Chorus earlier, *"The fiercest anger of all, the most incurable, / Is that which rages in the place of dearest love."*

We all know the old saying, Hell hath no fury like a woman scorned. As we have seen, at the heart of Medea's deep pain is insult and humiliation. The daughter of a king and a brilliant mother, and the granddaughter of a god, highly intelligent and very educated, capable and competent, she is a woman who knows things and who knows her value. The injury of betrayal and rejection, and the effrontery of total abandonment are intolerable to her. They are wholly unacceptable. After the critical and climactic confrontation between Medea and Jason, we watch as the dark forces of revenge take total possession of Medea.

After Jason leaves the scene, she says determinedly, *"It may be—/ And God uphold my words—that this your marriage-day / Will end with marriage lost / loathing and horror left."* From now on, as we shall see, Medea will focus only on finding the one way that she can most irreparably damage and ruin Jason, as she says, even if it kills her. This is where in the play I believe she decides she will murder his sons.

Broken promises and thwarted expectations, insult and humiliation, traps and shackles, alienation and exile, poverty, dependency, and the loss of personal dignity and opportunity—these are elements which can combine to incite in a woman terrible anger, violence, and the fierce desire to destroy.

During a Choral interlude, while the Corinthian Women are speaking reflectively about the hazards of sexual passion, Medea briefly leaves the scene to do what she has to do to get ready for her next move. She comes back again and listens when they are talking together about the vicissitudes of being without a homeland or friends.

Suddenly, unexpectedly, Aegeus, the king of Athens, appears. He is traveling through Corinth on his return from a visit to Delphi, and he is clearly delighted to meet up with Medea, and she with him. It turns out they are old friends. Creon was right; Medea has a reputation. And Jason meant it when he said Medea's gifts were widely recognized. This scene is important for several reasons. Obviously, it moves the plot along, but it also underscores the credibility of Medea, showing her in a positive peer relationship with a powerful man who admires her, and who appreciates her brain.

And there is *Eros* in this scene! Comfortably, Aegeus confides to Medea as to a respected friend that he has been to visit the oracle of Apollo to ask for children. Medea is empathetic and she tells him that she can help him. Then, with genuine regard, Aegeus notices that Medea is *"looking pale and wasted."* When she informs him that this very morning Jason has put another wife in her place, Aegeus is shocked: *"But such a thing is shameful,"* he cries.

This is feedback from an important man, the king of Athens himself—Athens which, in Euripides' time, was to Greece what Greece was to the rest of the world, the cradle of Western Civilization. Aegeus knows the history of this couple and he is incredulous that Jason has dared to do this. Acknowledging that Jason is indeed *"a bad lot,"* he goes as far as to advise Medea to *"let him go,"* uttering the usual collective opinion that men do these things. However, when she further informs him that because of Jason's worldly ambitions, she has not only been displaced at her own table, but has been banished from Corinth as well, Aegeus is totally appalled. To make a long story short, Medea and Aegeus make a deal. She promises to give him herbs to put an end to his apparent sterility and he, under oath (for Medea still believes in oaths and, as we shall see, so does Euripides), promises to give her sanctuary and lifetime protection in Athens.

The scene between Medea and Aegeus is crucial on several levels. We see that not only does Medea have the support of her servants and of her neighbors, but she also has the support of Aegeus, the king of the city that in fifth century BC was the political and cultural capital of the Greek world. Euripides' audience knew that. The contract that Medea makes with Aegeus gives her wiggle room. Her back is no longer firmly against an unyielding wall. Now Medea has a way out for herself, and for her children. She has safe passage to go to a place where she will be acknowledged and appreciated.

By the end of Aegeus' visit, Medea is reminded that she is in fact not totally bereft of friends in the world, and that there is a place where she can find a home again, and be welcomed and respected. Athens meant something. It was a good place where she could start anew, find community, raise her children, and do her particular kind of work. When Aegeus leaves Corinth, all Medea needs to do is get herself and her two children safely to Athens. We, the audience, can say with Aegeus, in so many words, let Jason go, Medea. Cut your losses. This husband of yours is not the man you thought he was. There's another chance for you out there—a great opportunity, in fact. Life goes on.

When Aegeus leaves the scene, Medea is not trapped anymore; she has been given a choice. At least that is what we might imagine.

I wonder if Andrea Yates of Texas knew she had a way out somewhere, somehow, before she methodically drowned her five small children in the family bathtub? Or did Susan

Smith of South Carolina know she had a choice before she pushed the family car into a lake with her two children in it? When I hear someone say, "Well, he had a choice, didn't he?", or, "Well, it was her choice," or, "You made your choice, after all," I really wonder if these are always fair questions, if often choice has nothing to do with it at all.

When "Jungians" say with a flair, "Oh, it's archetypal," what do we actually mean by that? Something takes us from behind, we say. Consciousness lapses. Unconscious forces take over. Do we always know what we are doing when we are caught up in an overwhelming *complex*, or when we are in the grip of powerful archetypal energy? Is there a choice about what we do? Is there any help for us? As Jung has said, "The archetype corresponding to the situation is activated, and as a result, those explosive and dangerous forces hidden in the archetype come into action, frequently with unpredictable consequences."[22]

I am suggesting that Euripides' powerful tragedy of a woman's revenge and retaliation against a man who rejects and abandons her gives us a graphic example and demonstration of what we are talking about, what we mean when we say that archetypal energy takes over a personality, that an archetype is ruling a life.

---

[22] "The Concept of the Collective Unconscious," CW 9i, par. 98.

Jung also said, "There is no lunacy people under the domination of an archetype will not fall prey to."[23] Terry Barton, the forest ranger in Colorado, who deliberately set the woods around Denver on fire and caused millions of dollars of damage—by the time she actually did that, did she have a choice? Or Andrea Yates, who drowned her five young children, one by one—by the time she did that, did she have a choice? Did the woman who ran over her philandering husband with the car until he was dead have a choice? Did my analysand, the very respectable, professional Edith, have a choice when she flew at her husband's throat and, if she could have in that instant, would have strangled him to death? Was she making a *conscious* choice? To repeat Jung's words, "There is no lunacy people under the domination of an archetype will not fall prey to."

Sadly, in Euripides' drama it becomes clear that for Medea the moment for choice has passed. Aegeus provides her with an escape route that guarantees she will not have to lose her own life if she does what, by this time, she knows she is going to do. Didn't she make him take an oath that he would protect her? Even though Athens had an open-door policy—meaning anyone could pass through—was it possible that, if he had any idea of what she actually already had in mind, Aegeus might have thought twice before promising and swearing to give her

_____

23   Ibid.

sanctuary? Now Medea can safely complete her plan of vengeance and reprisal with impunity. She will do what will bring Jason to his knees. She will poison Glauce and Creon, and then, no matter how difficult—and it will be terribly difficult for her—she will destroy the fruits of her love for Jason, and of their union—she will kill their two sons. And by doing that she will effectively kill Jason, finish him, end his line and *"the House of Jason."*

With the visit of Aegeus, the final piece falls into place and the horrors can begin. Does the darkest side of Medea, the deepest shadow, take over? Is it psychopathy? Psychosis? Jung's words again: "The pathological element does not lie in the existence of these (monstrous) ideas, but in the dissociation of consciousness that can no longer control the unconscious."[24]

In the course of Euripides' drama, we watch as prodigious anger, envy, lust, and pride slowly and gradually possess this woman's personality. We watch as normal and healthy emotional reactions, powerful emotional reactions to seriously troubling and unhappy human events, turn into unconscionable evil deeds. The infernal archetypal machinery that has been lurching in place starts to roll at a ghastly pace. Medea becomes the Terrible Mother.

After Aegeus' visit, Medea spells out her entire dire plan to the Women of Corinth, and then sends the Nurse

---

24   "Archetypes of the Collective Unconscious," CW 9i, par. 83.

to call Jason back. When he returns, she puts on an act for him. Medea apologizes profusely for her previous attitude, and gets Jason to agree to let their children offer gifts of reconciliation to Glauce on her behalf. We soon hear the good news from the Tutor, when he returns from accompanying the children to the palace, that the princess has embraced the young boys and accepted Medea's dazzlingly beautiful gifts. For the Chorus, as well as for the audience, the suspense is terrible. We all know that the headdress and the gown that Medea sent to Glauce have been treated with a deadly poison.

Alas, soon enough, the Messenger arrives with the bad news. We learn that Glauce has died a horrible death, and that King Creon, in his attempt to save his only daughter's life, has also grotesquely succumbed to the poison's burning havoc. By the time Jason arrives at his home prepared to get his revenge for these crimes, Medea has already killed their two children offstage.

In the final scene of Euripides' drama, Medea is revealed on the point of flight—the two boys' bloodied bodies lying beside her in the dragon-drawn chariot which Helios, the sun god, has miraculously provided for her last-minute deliverance to Athens. As difficult as this may be to take in at first, for Euripides, Medea's impunity is underscored by a god! Before she disappears, Medea has the satisfaction of knowing that she is leaving Jason behind, thoroughly broken, and she has the bitter foreknowledge that, when his time comes, the man who was once her hero will die an inglorious death, *". . . (his) head shattered / By a timber from the Argo's hull . . ."*

Before I end my reading of Euripides' *Medea*, there are a few details I would like to go over with a finer comb. In the last section of the drama, which is called the *denouement*, the unraveling, it is interesting to note the role of the Nurse. The old woman leaves the stage early, shortly after the arrival of the Chorus. Remember, at the request of the Corinthian women, she goes into the palace to ask Medea to come out and speak to them. We do not see the Nurse again until after Aegeus departs for Athens. It is when Medea is telling the Women of her terrible plan that the Nurse quietly reappears.

When Medea explains to them what she is going to do, the Chorus is clearly appalled. Stage directions read *"(the Nurse) listens in silence."* Then Medea says, *"Nurse! You are the one I use for messages of trust. / Go and bring Jason here. As you're a loyal servant, / And a woman, breathe no word about my purposes."* The Nurse knows what is going to happen. We could say she almost predicted it, for after the Tutor told her that Creon was going to banish Jason's sons from Corinth as well as their mother, she could not believe that Jason would allow this to happen. Remember, she says, *"Then we're lost, if we must add new trouble / To old, before we're rid of what we had already."* We recall that the Nurse had to keep herself from cursing Jason. Now, she does not refuse the orders of her Mistress. She stands firmly on Medea's side, and does her bidding.

The loyal servant is a convention in classical drama, as is the use of masks. The solidarity between servant and master suggests a *shadowy* connection. To me it's interesting to speculate that, since there is no actual dialogue between the Nurse and Medea in the whole play, both major female speaking roles in Medea were performed by the same actor. We could say that ultimately the old woman is in silent collusion with Medea's ghastly plot. She goes to fetch Jason as she is told to do and, obviously, she does not warn him of what she knows is in store. Is this the rebellion of the inner-slave, the *shadow* of the foreign woman who has concretely tried to know her place and be obedient, but in truth deeply resents the fact that she is expected to be submissive and agreeable? As we learned before, in Euripides' world, neither women nor slaves nor foreigners had any legal rights. Does the slave, inner and outer, finally get her opportunity for revenge? There are no more directions to bring the Nurse back on stage after she goes off to fetch Jason.

Also interesting to me in the *denouement* of this tragedy, in the awful unfolding of events at the end of the play, is how eager, whether on or off stage, the different characters are to hear what they want to hear. For example, there's the children's Tutor, a cynical fellow we met in the second scene of the play, who says to the old woman who is the

Nurse, *"What man's not guilty? It's taken you a long time to learn / That everybody loves himself more than his neighbor. / These boys are nothing to their father; he's in love."* The Tutor is the one who accompanies his charges with Jason to visit Princess Glauce. He then reports back about what appeared to be a heartwarming meeting between Glauce and Jason's children. In spite of everything he knows about Medea, and Jason, and regardless of everything he has heard and seen and said before, he is filled with joy and hope for what appears to be a reconciliation. Is hope the *shadow* of cynicism?

Ultimately, despite everything Creon and Jason and Glauce know and fear about Medea, her history, her reputation, her dark gifts, they each allow themselves to be charmed by her. They simply want to hear what they want to hear in order to justify their own venal motives and actions. With eyes wide open (or eyes wide shut?), one by one they each fall into Medea's by this time well-calculated trap.

In his death agony, we can imagine that Creon lived long enough to choke on his last words to Medea: *"You can hardly in one day accomplish what I am afraid of."* Never underestimate the power of a woman. As I suggested earlier, Creon was worried about what people would think. He did not want to go down in history as an unreasonable man. And, with the Chorus listening in the background, Creon let his *ego* get in the way of his instinct.

When Medea calls Jason back, she knows exactly what he wants to hear. She makes him look good and herself look bad. By pretending to peaceably acquiesce to his will, she is letting Jason off the hook, which is what he wanted and had the temerity to expect from her in the first place. Jason says in his typically patronizing tones:

> *I am pleased Medea,*
> *That you have changed your mind; though indeed I do*
> *   not blame*
> *Your first resentment. Only naturally a woman*
> *Is angry when her husband marries a second wife.*
> *You have had wiser thoughts; and though it has taken time,*
> *You have recognized the right decision.*
> *This is the act*
> *Of a sensible woman.*

To Jason's great relief, it looks like Medea is not being difficult anymore. She is being obedient, and he can now justify his betrayal of her, his rejection and abandonment of the woman who saved his life, and who gave him sons, without any guilt feelings—much less any sense of responsibility. Alas, his machismo gets in the way of his common sense.

There is one moment when he has a qualm—but for the wrong reason. He tells Medea that she needn't send Glauce any gifts:

But why deprive yourself of such things, foolish woman?
(Jason is really incorrigible. Two minutes ago she
   was a "sensible woman"! He says,)
Do you think a royal palace is in want of dresses?
If my wife values me at all she will yield to Me
More than to costly presents . . .

But Medea continues to charm him with humble words:
"*Don't stop me. Gifts, they say, persuade even the gods; / . . . To buy / My sons from exile I would give life, not just gold.*"

Indeed, later, according to the Messenger's report, Jason did have to persuade Glauce to receive his and Medea's children in her room at the palace. Apparently, Glauce's immediate instinctive reaction on their arrival was to frown and look away, but, the young bride, not wanting to displease her new husband, went along with his wishes. She was obedient. And indeed, as Medea knew she would be, Glauce was easily won over by the wonderful presents. As the Messenger describes it, Jason and the two boys had hardly left the room before Glauce took "*The embroidered gown and put it round her.*"

Then she placed
Over her curls the golden coronet, and began
To arrange her hair in a bright mirror, smiling at
Her lovely form reflected there. Then she stood up,
And to and fro stepped daintily about the room
On white bare feet, and many times she would twist back
To see how the dress fell in clear folds to the heel.

And this was just minutes before her pitiable demise, which the Messenger then describes in horrible detail. The dress had been soaked in a poison that upon contact devoured her flesh.

We can assume that when Glauce married Jason, she was doing what her father told her to do. However, Jason, being the handsome, glamorous, experienced older man he was—surely Glauce was not averse to the political arrangement these fatherly men were making for her. As Medea says to Jason at the very end, "*. . . The Princess was wrong too, and so / Was Creon, when he took you for his son-in-law / And thought he could exile me with impunity.*"

Like Creon, like Jason, Glauce knew Medea's history and reputation, and she had to have heard about Medea's curses on her and the royal family. Poor immature and obedient Glauce stumbled into the *shadowy* snare of her own youthful ambition, and of her vanity.

After the Messenger exits, the Chorus chants, "*Today we see the will of Heaven, blow after blow. / Bring down on Jason justice and calamity.*"

Medea tells the Women of Corinth that she is now going to do the unspeakable thing: She is going to kill her children. She knows that they will be murdered sooner or later in any case, that because of what she has done (that is, murder Glauce and Creon) her two boys will never be safe anywhere, least of all in Corinth. Therefore, she will kill them now with her own hands.

Of course, we know, and the women of Corinth know, and Medea knows, that her motives for killing the two children are more complicated and darker than that. Even before the arrival of the Messenger with the bitter news about Glauce and Creon, Medea says, *"I understand / The horror of what I am going to do; but anger / The spring of all life's horror, masters my resolve."* At the source of this anger is the force of the archetype.

The stage direction reads, Medea *goes into the house.* With a chill we realize what is about to happen. The Corinthian Women call on the Earth to awaken. They call on the Sun to stop her. The blood of a god is flowing in these children's veins; what is about to happen cannot be! But it is happening. In the background we can hear the boys screaming for help.

"Stone and iron you are," says the Chorus of Medea. *"What can be strange or terrible after this?"* What can be strange or terrible after Andrea Yates systematically drowned her five children in the family bathtub, one by one? Apparently, when his turn came, the eldest, who was seven years old, saw what his mother was doing, and he fought her. She had to struggle with him to the very end to hold his head under the water until he was dead. His seven-year-old resistance to his mother's archetypal Medea energy was in vain.

In the final moments of Euripides' tragedy, Jason, running and breathless, enters the scene. He has seen what happened to Glauce and Creon and is determined—before it is too late—to rescue his children from the vengeance of the rest of the royal family. When the Chorus tells him what has already occurred, he screams he will kill Medea.

Too late. It is at this moment that Medea appears safely, as the stage directions read, *above the roof, sitting in a chariot drawn by dragons, with the bodies of her two dead children beside her.* And she wastes no time letting Jason know that the Sun has sent this chariot pulled by two dragons. Her grandfather Helios has sent the *Deus ex machina* to save her from the hands of her enemies.

In this very last scene of the tragedy, there are more recriminations back and forth between Medea and Jason, and there is more name-calling and blaming. Jason, now for the first time overcome with emotion, cries out that he never should have married Medea in the first place, that he always knew she was a bad person. Incredulously and contemptuously, he accuses her of murdering their sons *"out of mere sexual jealousy."* Medea replies very calmly:

> *. . . Zeus the father of all*
> *Knows well what service I once rendered you, and how*
> *You have repaid me. You were mistaken if you thought*
> *You could dishonour my bed and live a pleasant life*
> *And laugh at me...*

Hurl at me
What names you please! I've reached your heart; and
that is right.

She tells him it was his insult to her in taking a new wife that killed their sons. He tells her that it was her problem because she was not a modest woman. A modest woman, he says, would not have behaved as if the whole world were lost just because her husband slept with someone else.

Still, Jason genuinely grieves at the spectacle of his dead children. Medea has reached Jason's heart. Before she departs, though, she reminds him, and we remember, that just a little while earlier he was totally in accord with Creon's decree to banish her, and the two boys with her, to a life of poverty and degradation, and danger. He didn't really care what happened to any of them. Medea says, *"Now you have loving words, now kisses for them: / Then you disowned them, sent them into exile."*

Jason is finally really feeling; he is suffering. Yes. But to the very end, he accuses Medea, blames her for her deeds. Not once does he make the connection between his behavior, his words and his attitudes, and her reaction and response. Jason believes he is a man who has been grievously wronged. What has happened has happened because Medea got angry—because Medea is and always was a bad person.

There is no reconciliation between Medea and Jason. To the very end, Medea and Jason, and the *masculine* and *feminine* principles of life which they embody and represent, remain polarized. There is no easy back and forth. No creative polarity develops between them. No integration. To the very end, what has happened to Medea is Jason's fault. To the very end, what has happened to Jason is Medea's fault. There is no container for the tension of opposites; everything falls apart.

The chariot of Helios drawn by the power of the Great Goddess suggests another story as well. Jason never recognizes that Medea his wife, Medea the woman, embodies a divine principle. He never acknowledges the divine *feminine*. Helios does! In Euripides' interpretation of this myth, the sun god, Helios, knows that Medea is a goddess abused.

While Jason continues to bemoan his lot, Medea, finished with her regrets and recriminations, rides off in her chariot of Earth and Sun. As she leaves, she tells us that, before she goes to receive sanctuary in Athens, she will first visit the temple of Hera Acraea to bury her children, and to ensure that on these sacred grounds their remains will not be violated. Medea knows what she has done.

Andrea Yates knew what she did. After she drowned her five children, one by one, she called the police. In 2002 she was sentenced to life in prison. The conviction was reversed by an appeals court in 2005. Yates was retried in 2006 and found not guilty by reason of insanity, and sent to a Texas mental hospital for the rest of her life. What opportunities has she had for the ritual expiation of her desperate acts?

Medea tells us that she is going to *"…ordain an annual feast and sacrifice / To be solemnized forever by the people of Corinth, / To expiate this impious murder."* The Chorus has the last word:

> *Many are the Fates which Zeus in Olympus dispenses.*
> *Many matters the gods bring to surprising ends.*
> *The things we thought would happen do not happen;*
> *The unexpected God makes possible;*
> *And such is the conclusion of this story.*

Disappointment, broken promises, thwarted expectations, insult and humiliation, physical abuse, the feeling of being trapped and stuck, and on top of all that alienation and exile, poverty, dependency, and the loss of personal dignity and opportunity—these are elements that can combine to excite in a woman anger, violence, and the impulse to destroy.

PART TWO

Streams of the sacred rivers flow uphill;

Tradition, order, all things are reversed:

Deceit is men's device now,

Men's oaths are god's dishonor.

—Euripides, *Medea*

HISTORICAL AND CULTURAL BACKGROUND

Before returning to Euripides' tragedy, *Medea*, and to an examination of "Medea rage" and the Medea myth, I would like to add to a deeper and broader understanding of the significance of this play, by briefly exploring some of its historical and cultural background.

Studying a play has similarities to dream work. In fact, as Jung has pointed out, "...there are a great number of... dreams in which a definite structure can be perceived, not unlike that of a drama."[1] In Jungian analysis, when we are looking at a dream with our client, we don't only deal with the story or motif. There are many things going on at once. For example, we ask the dreamer, "What happened that day?" In order to go deeper, to go from what we call the *objective* level to the *subjective* level, we look closely at the details of the imagery and the symbols and, most importantly, ask for the dreamer's personal associations. To come up with a viable interpretation together, as analysts we need to be keenly aware of what is currently going on in our analysand's life, keeping in mind the early history and what seems to have been constellated archetypally in his or her psyche. We also need to be able to identify the *complexes.* A dream is embedded in a rich and many-layered context.

---

1   "On the Nature of Dreams," *The Structure and Dynamics of the Psyche,* CW 8, par. 561.

When doing a close reading of a classical Greek drama like Euripides' *Medea*, we first look carefully at the structure—at the Exposition and the Rising Action, the Climax and the *denouement*. It is very important to get the tone, to be able to hear the lines being spoken by the various characters, to hear the different voices. Reading a play which is meant to be seen and heard on a stage is a skill not unlike reading music. After a thorough, close reading we can retell the story in ordinary language and make an interpretation, but to really get at the playwright's deeper meaning—in other words, to get more out of it than the complexities of plot—more work has to be done. Like a dream, a great play is embedded in a rich and many-layered context.

Looking at the personal and individual level when we study Euripides' play, we also need to explore the more universal aspects of the piece. We certainly want to be able to recognize and identify different aspects of the "Medea rage" as it currently manifests itself in human life in "situations which might occur any day in any street in Athens" in fifth century BC.[2] However, to find the epiphany of truth in *Medea*, we also want to get closer to the Greek playwright's possibly more profound intentions in his own time, as well as to their timeless significance.

Most of the information we have about the conventions of the Golden Age of Greek Theater in Athens in the fifth

---

2   Philip Vellacott, "Introduction," *Alcestis and Other Plays*, 14.

century BC—when it appears full-blown on the stage of history—comes from inference from the plays themselves, from vase paintings, for example, and from writers of later centuries. Aristotle, the great collector and compiler of data in his time, wrote the *Poetics* 75 years after Euripides' death. Vetruvius wrote *De Architectura*, a detailed look at Greek and Roman architecture, shortly before the birth of Christ, and Pollux wrote *Onomastikon*, which included a lengthy discussion of Greek music and theater, in the second century AD. It seems there are no archeological remains in Greece of fifth century BC theaters, but we have a basic idea of the way the theater in Euripides' time looked from the still relatively intact structure built in the fourth century BC (that is, 365 BC) at Epidaurus.[3]

The most important thing to always keep in mind about the origins of theater in the Western world is that it developed from religious ritual. In Greece in archaic times, it supposedly started with a kind of collective and collaborative worship that included music and chanting and dancing. The occasion would have been a sacred fertility rite, for example, or a celebration of death and rebirth in nature to honor the Earth god, Dionysus. In the middle of the sixth century BC, Thespis, the first actor, emerged from an undifferentiated choral group. He could engage with the chorus as a separate entity. He could narrate; he

---

3   For information about classical Greek theater and playwrights, I am indebted to Phyllis Hartnoll, *A Concise History of the Theatre*, 7-31, and Macgowan & Melnitz, *Golden Ages of the Theater*, 1-20.

could perform. The theory is that it was around this time in Greece when the *dithyramb*, or choral hymn which was sung to Dionysus, became *drama*. Dionysus was the god of fertility and fecundity, and of the vine. The *dithyramb*— or group song that celebrated the story of Dionysus, the mortal child of Zeus who was dismembered and reborn again as a god—was gradually replaced by the stories of archaic culture heroes.

In 534 BC, Thespis, who is considered to be not only the first actor, but also the first dramatist and the first *trouper*, won the first Athenian prize for tragedy. Aeschylus, the first Greek tragedian whose work has survived, started writing his plays for one actor and a chorus. Eventually, by the fifth century BC, he introduced a second actor and, voila, we had dialogue. This is not unlike the origins of consciousness, as the one breaks up into two. More personalized different points of view could be expressed in a play; there could be opposition and conflict. You can't have drama without conflict. You can't have a real drama without two opposing forces clashing. The next tragedian whose works have survived was Sophocles, who introduced a third actor. When Euripides, a younger contemporary of Sophocles, came along, he also worked with three actors, but in his plays, the role of the chorus, although still very significant, was reduced from 50 to 15.

By the second half of the fifth century BC, with three actors and with the use of different masks, there could be many characters in a play and no end of staged complications. Euripides' characters and situations are considered to be more down to earth and recognizable than those of his two famous colleagues, Aeschylus and Sophocles. However, even though the plots of Euripides' plays can be interpreted more realistically, we still need to take into consideration how the historical background of the time in which they were written, as well as how the mechanics and the occasion of the classical Greek theater of the fifth century BC, were determining factors in the way the spectators could experience the drama on a level deeper and broader than the personal and individual. These spectators, after all, were acquainted with the stories, which originated in the ninth and eighth centuries BC.

What were the mechanics of the theater? We have already mentioned the chorus and the mask as conventions of the classical Greek stage. These elements are decidedly unrealistic. In Euripides' time, the main actors and members of the chorus wore masks, and to distinguish themselves, the main actors' masks were larger than those of the chorus; the large mouths in the masks are thought to have been used as megaphones. Padding their bodies and wearing long flowing robes (chiton) and platform shoes (cothurne), they were portraying larger-than-life characters, but they also had to be seen and heard from a great distance, for the plays were performed outdoors, usually in a beautiful setting where two hillsides came together and where there was a natural hollowed out circular playing area at the bottom.

What about the occasion? Every year in Athens there were two major religious festivals dedicated to the god Dionysus. The most important one, which took place in late March to early April, was a week-long religious and civic holiday called City Dionysia. This festival must have dated back at least to the middle of the sixth century BC (534 BC), when Thespis won the first Athenian prize for tragedy. Attendance at the City Dionysia seems to have been like a kind of Easter duty. Everyone was expected to go; those who couldn't afford it were subsidized. During the celebration, plays were performed for three consecutive days, and Athenians and Greeks by the thousands sat on the hillsides and watched the performances. The annual playwriting competition was the high point of the festival.

After roughly 2,500 years, 33 works by three classical Greek tragedians—Aeschylus, Sophocles, and Euripides—have survived. Aeschylus wrote 90 plays and won 13 first prizes. Seven of his works have survived. Sophocles is supposed to have written more than 100 plays. He won 18 first prizes, but only eight of his tragedies survive. It is said that Euripides wrote 92 plays. He won five first prizes; we still have 19 of his works. We may imagine that the plays that were preserved over the centuries were not only the winners of the annual play-writing contests, but also were among the most popular and/or most controversial plays of their time. These were the plays that continued to be interesting to audiences in the Hellenistic period that came between the Hellenic Greeks and the Romans, and which much later were carried from Constantinople to Italy during the Turkish invasion in 1453, when their appearance spurred the flowering of the Italian Renaissance.

Fifth century BC Athens was the center of the civilized world. However, the archaic origins of the theater as religious ritual and collective worship were still strongly manifested during the celebration of the City Dionysia. At the center of the playing area, always visible, was the altar dedicated to the nature god, Dionysus. Interestingly, the word "tragedy" comes from the Greek words *tragos* for goat and *ode* for song. We know that during the festival, in the Comedy which followed each of the three days' three Tragedies, the comic actors wore large symbolic phalluses as part of their costumes to emphasize the theater's ancient origins and the devotion to the god of fertility. In these ancient Dionysian rites, the goat was a sacrificial animal, and in the so-called satyr plays, or burlesques that ended the festivities of the City Dionysia, the actors representing the god above and the animal below wore goat-skins.

Early and late in fifth century BC Athens, the City Dionysia was a celebration of the mystery of the sacrificial death of Dionysus, and of his transformation and rebirth. Apparently, the greatest poetry in Greece was written to honor Dionysus, and actors—who received subsidies from the government—were considered his servants. Over time, the tragedies dealt with the Homeric myths and heroic legends, all the old stories, but they were still performed in honor of the Earth god. These dramatic productions became the most important and exciting feature of the annual holiday and of the worship of Dionysus.

EURIPIDES' PLACE IN GREEK THEATRE IN FIFTH CENTURY BC

Briefly and schematically, I am providing a little more detail about Euripides and about the historical period he experienced and witnessed growing up.

Euripides died in exile in 407 BC. It is speculated that had he not left Athens and gone to Macedonia to live when he was 70, his fate would not have been unlike that of the famous teacher, Socrates, who was 15 years younger.[4] Euripides has been referred to as "the bad boy of Athenian drama."[5] In his time, this prolific and prize-winning playwright was considered to be an iconoclast and a dangerous man. He used the stage and the conventional tragic form of his day as his vehicle for challenging orthodox assumptions.

According to English classical scholar Philip Vellacott, in Euripides' view of life, his central belief was—and it is very important to remember this when we talk about his plays, and particularly when we talk about *Medea*— that "the world and human nature held impersonal forces

---

4   Philip Vellacott, "Introduction," *Alcestis*, 10.
5   See Daniel Mendelsohn, *The New York Review of Books*, Feb. 13, 2003.

of terrifying power which, once set in motion, (could) cause unlimited suffering."[6] In Euripides' tragic vision, or *Weltanshauung*, these cosmic forces brought havoc to the innocent as well as the guilty. Dispassionate powers represented by Aphrodite, Artemis, Hermes, Dionysus, or Apollo, could be recognized at work, for example, in irrational and violent outbursts of anger or sexual desire, feelings of revenge or lust for power—outbursts which were devastating to individuals and communities alike. (Two of Euripides' tragedies, *The Women of Troy* and *Helen*, deal with the horrors of the Trojan War.) In Jungian psychology we might call these forces archetypes. Euripides would certainly have been in agreement with Jung's 20th century statement that there is no lunacy people under the domination of an archetype will not fall prey to. According to Vellacott, although Zeus was always considered to be in the background, the father of gods and men, mysterious and unknowable, "the given, unquestioned Divinity behind every manifestation, the Unity of the supernatural world," Euripides, like Socrates, publicly called into question the whole establishment of the Olympian pantheon.[7]

Born in 484 BC, there really is not too much known about Euripides' early life. He was reputed to be a very learned man with a famous library, and was friends with some of the most outstanding intellectuals and artists of

---

6 Unless otherwise noted, for historical information about Euripides' life, I have consulted Vellacott's "Introduction," in *Alcestis and Other Plays*, 7-16.

7 Ibid., 12.

his day. His career as a playwright started shortly before he was 50 years old; *Medea* was his first tragedy and his second play. *The Bacchae*, his last and most famous tragedy, was written while he was living in exile, and produced posthumously. Over a period of roughly 20 years, during the last third of his life, Euripides wrote 92 plays. Remember, he only won five first prizes at the festivals of the City Dionysia; 19 of his plays have survived.

Born around the time of the famous sea battle of Salamis (480 BC), when the power of the Persian invaders of the Greek peninsula was finally broken, Euripides lived in a fascinating age. During his first 50 years, the free alliance of Greek maritime states converted to an Athenian empire. When he was a small child, after many years of war and occupation, the city of Athens was finally being rebuilt. He was there when Athens became the political and cultural center of the Mediterranean world. Literally, Euripides grew up in the cradle of civilization and, from the very beginning, he was part of the first serious political experiment with democracy in the history of the world. Alas, as he grew older, he discovered that building an empire is not only about civilizing, but also about accumulating wealth and economic advantage—and about manipulating and maintaining power.

Greece, then a tiny nation about the size of Miami,[8] was composed of some 10,000 men, their wives, children

---

[8]   See Harper Collins, *Atlas of World History*, Ann Arbor, MI: Borders Press,1989, 74-75.

and other dependents, as well as "metics" or outsiders (foreigners), and slaves.[9] During the first two-thirds of Euripides' life, he witnessed the suppression of Asian barbarianism, the establishment of order, and the rule of law (which Jason was so boastful about). He witnessed as well the flourishing of architecture, poetry, and philosophy. Human values and ideas that have endured in some parts of the world into our own day—and, for better or for worse, that in some parts of the world many still cherish—were conceived and brought forth in the Golden Age of Greece during which Euripides lived. Some scholars believe that there has been nothing else quite like this 50-year period of human history.

However, at around the age of 50, when Euripides started writing plays and wrote *Medea*, Greek society was becoming more and more paradoxical. Serious contradictions were emerging on the home front, as some "democratic" ideals were turning into conventionality and rigid conformity. So-called law-and-order was getting in the way of naturalness and spontaneity, and human nature. As we see in *Medea*, it was also getting in the way of oaths and honor.

In some quarters, numbers were considered to be more attractive than the physical world. The Pythagorean Brotherhood, for example, held that the ultimate nature of the universe was mathematical and numerical, despite

---

9   Vellacott, *Alcestis and Other Plays*, 7.

physical evidence to the contrary. Historian, J.M. Roberts points out that this had ultimate repercussions "in a view of the universe which, because it was constructed on mathematical and deductive principles, rather than from observation, fixed astronomy on the wrong lines for nearly two thousand years."[10] That is, until Copernicus (1473-1543) and his deathbed publication in 1543 of *On the Revolutions of the Celestial Spheres* challenged the entire system of ancient authority and ultimately, as we know, required a complete change in the philosophical conception of the universe. When, almost 100 years later (1632), Galileo, who was the first to look at the heavens through a telescope, defended the Copernican system (*Dialogue Concerning the Two Chief World Systems*), the classical idea that man was the center of the universe was so strongly held, the Jesuit Inquisition condemned him to house arrest for the rest of his life (d. 1637).

Another thing was going on in the world around him as Euripides was growing older. Traces of asceticism were gradually beginning to appear in the thought of the time (Plato, c. 427- 347). For example, there was the idea that "man is irreconcilably divided between the soul of divine origin and the body which imprisons it," or, in other words, that man is divided between spirit and matter. Not reconciliation or integration, but the domination of the one

---

10   For information about Euripides' times, also see *The Hutchinson History of the World*, 195-221.

by the other had to be the outcome of the struggle. As
historian Roberts observes, "It was an idea which would
pass into Christianity with enormous effect."[11]

Also, under the tent of "democracy," oligarchy and
tyranny were emerging. Some would say that Greek
democracy was actually an extended oligarchy in the first
place, since it was mostly run by certain powerful families,
and since slaves as well as women and foreigners had no
legal or political rights. Abroad, the Greek "democratic"
ideals were turning into expansionism and imperialism;
rivalries and tensions between Athens and Sparta were
coming to a head. In fact, Euripides actually wrote *Medea*
one year before the outbreak of aggression and violence
that we know as the Peloponnesian Wars (431-404 BC),
which lasted 27 years. In other words, he wrote his first
tragedy in a time of military buildup and in a time of the
theoretical suppression of nature and of humane values.

As Jung has pointed out, "Civilization does not consist
in progress as such and in mindless destruction of the
old values, but in developing and refining the good that
has been won."[12] Remember when Euripides has Medea
say to Jason, *"Do you, I wonder, think that the old gods / No
longer rule? Or that new laws are now in force?"* Her words
are like a warning, for as we said earlier, in Euripides'

---

11   See *Hutchinson*, 237-238.
12   "A Psychological Approach to the Trinity," *Psychology and Religion: West*,
CW 11, par. 292.

tragic vision of life, the gods represented irrepressible cosmic forces. Once set in motion, these dispassionate and impersonal powers—not unlike what we call archetypal energy—could cause unlimited suffering to individuals and communities alike, the innocent as well as the guilty.

During the last 20 years of his life, Euripides watched as liberal hopes gave way to imperial realities and the horrors of war. In his dramas he gave witness to the gradual breakdown of what has come to be called the Golden Age of Greece, and of Athens' ultimate loss of its political and cultural leadership in the Mediterranean world. Euripides' critics did not like what they saw in the dramatic mirror he held up to them and to Athenian society. After all, we may (or may not) know we are hypocrites, but we don't like being told or shown we are on the public stage in a serious play. There, we like to see our ideal self and how we want others to see us. Even if we don't really believe in the gods anymore, we don't say so openly, for it's just the outer show we want to have presented on the stage, the *persona*. Our *shadow* side we would rather see projected on someone else—or somewhere else. No wonder Euripides in his old age had to flee Athens for his life. He wrote his last and reputedly greatest play, *The Bacchae*, which is thematically related to *Medea*, while he was in exile. He died before it was produced.

In the last three decades of the fifth century BC, all of Greece was shaken by the Peloponnesian Wars. Perhaps, as if to compensate for the chaos of war that was happening around them, there was something else going on among Athenian intellectuals around the time Euripides was turning 50. It was called the Sophistic Movement. As the famous historian of Greek theater, H.D.F. Kitto, has put it, "It is as if the Greek mind, during this period, began to shift its weight from one leg to another: from intuitive intelligence, based on observation and on reflection about human experience, and expressing itself through art and the traditional imagery of mythology, to a conscious, calculated analysis of experience which made use of new intellectual techniques…"[13] We might say that certain kinds of rigidly one-sided and therefore psychologically inferior *masculine* attitudes were starting to dominate and diminish significant *feminine* ones. In Kitto's opinion, great poetry in Greece—that is, poetry which deals with major issues of human life—dies with Euripides and Sophocles.

In the second half of the fifth century BC, Sophists, who were using these new intellectual techniques, represented a class of professional teachers of philosophy and rhetoric who were especially known for their ingenuity and speciousness in argumentation. Today we define sophistry as "a subtle, tricky, superficially plausible, but generally fallacious method of reasoning."[14] In other words, *sophistry* means a false argument. It looks good or sounds good, but it really doesn't have a lot of merit or substance

---

13   *Greek Tragedy,* 187-188.
14   *The Random House College Dictionary: Revised Edition,* 1975.

and, most importantly, its purpose is to deceive or defeat. In his tragedy *Hippolytus*, Euripides has one of his characters say that he speaks with his lips, but not with his heart. Remember that in Jason's confrontation with Medea, his argument to excuse himself from his behind-her-back betrayal is that he married the princess to ensure their social and economic security.

As Jung reminds us, "Culture means continuity, not a tearing up of roots through 'progress.'"[15] Euripides started writing his plays and tragedies at the historical moment in classical Greece when political, intellectual, and social directions were rapidly and radically changing. In an expansionist and imperialistic mode, his "democratic" country was preparing for war with Sparta. There was an intellectual movement afoot which fostered a training in dispute, whose purpose was to support deception with words and to encourage argument for the sake of winning, rather than for the sake of communication and attaining truthfulness. As a rigid austerity was starting to enter the thought of the time, a repressive lid was being put on real and inescapable forces of life—or, as Vellacott puts it, "on the passions which are in human blood and will obey their own laws."[16] In his plays and tragedies, Euripides was an outspoken critic of his time. Azar Nafisi, the contemporary Iranian writer, puts it persuasively: "Every great work of

---

15   "The Gifted Child," *The Development of Personality*, CW 17, par. 250.
16   Vellacott, "Introduction," 9.

art . . . is . . . an act of insubordination against the betrayals, horrors and infidelities of life."[17]

THE TRUTH OF MEDEA FOR THE GREEKS

So, what deep truth is being celebrated here in this great dramatic work, *Medea*, about a man's betrayal of his wife, and a woman's horrible revenge? What is the epiphany of truth in Euripides' tragedy? What was the divine revelation that Euripides was bringing to his audiences at the City Dionysia at the beginning of the last third of fifth century BC Athens, that is still valid and profoundly relevant for audiences today?

I've tried to give a little more detail about the playwright's background, and about what was happening in the collective consciousness of the time in which he was living. And I hope you will have a better sense of the kind of theater for which Euripides was writing.

As mentioned earlier, the classical Greek theater of the fifth century BC was an outgrowth and an extension of what originally was a worship service, a religious ritual honoring the Earth god, Dionysus—the god of life and death, the god of light and dark. During a historical period focused on subduing nature and creating civilization,

---

17   *Reading Lolita in Tehran: A Memoir in Books,* 3, 47.

perhaps the City Dionysia was officially sponsored and organized like a kind of Mardi Gras, a carnival or safety valve to give approved but restricted expression a few times a year for the people to experience and honor the other side of life. After all, Dionysus was the god of laughter, of the joy of life and spontaneity. He was the god of the fullness of life. He was also the god of the irrational, of ecstasy and ecstatic frenzy.

We may not forget that theater grew out of a devotion honoring the Earth, and that Dionysus was the god who presided over the mystery of living and dying and being reborn—again and again. Dionysus presided over the changing cycles of nature, the dark winter and the bright spring. He was the god of dancing and singing and music. As Demeter was the goddess of bread and of milk and honey, Dionysus was the god of wine. Last but not least, he was the lord of women, who, after all, carry the mystery of life and death and the changes of the seasons in their own bodies. Despite the official attention to self-control and law-and-order, and to attitudes which supported austerity and sophistry, was the annual City Dionysia in Euripides' time an acknowledgement of the existence of what Dionysus represented in all his aspects?

In Greece, ruins and well-preserved monuments— huge, hewn out of granite and marble, every measurement precise—stand in remote and wild and rocky places. Built after the defeat of the Persians in the battle of Salamis during a time when barbarism was supposedly being subdued by civilization, do these impressive man-made edifices appear to be striving to dominate their unmanageable natural environment? When he turned 50, Euripides was living in a period when we might say there was an effort going on, if not exactly to control nature, certainly to give it less value.

Against the historical background of Euripides, and on the altar to Dionysus that functions as a stage, with these larger-than-life characters and passions, how in *Medea* is the playwright holding up a critical mirror to his time? What is the deeper meaning, the epiphany of truth in *Medea* that goes beyond what is happening every day on any street in Athens, that is, the situation of a woman being rejected and abandoned by the man she loves—a very hurt and angry woman—who gets her revenge through violence?

In the big picture, Medea and Jason represent opposite poles—opposite values—opposites. Any too much or too little is a negative. Symbolically, Jason represents *masculine* values, positive ones as well as inferior ones. Logos. He takes initiative, risks; he is adventurous and ambitious. With a goal in mind, he makes a plan, focuses on it and arrives at the steps he needs to take to achieve it. Supposedly, Jason was the first European hero to embark on a challenging and dangerous journey.[18] Medea represents *feminine* values, for good and for bad. *Eros.* Feeling

---

18   Edith Hamilton, *Mythology*, 17.

values that have to do with relationship and emotion—with receiving, containing and holding—with spontaneity, creative imagination and humor.

Remember the imaginative ways Medea helped Jason to keep safe in the final and decisive phase of his search for the Golden Fleece? Remember too that she gave him the ointment to apply all over his body and his weapons so that he would not be wounded? What stronger protection, what greater balm, what better weapon can a man have when he enters the battle of life, the fateful dragon fight, than to know that he is loved by a woman who is not his mother?

Medea possesses the extraordinary gift of creative fantasy. She is comfortable with improvisation as well as with the irrational world. For love she went out of her way to help Jason achieve the object of his heroic quest. During the first period of their association, Jason and Medea appeared to complement each other. Masculine and Feminine, Eros and Logos, Yin and Yang. *Anima* and *Animus* worked together as a team.

When we meet him in the play, perhaps not unlike Greek civilization in the last third of the fifth century BC, Jason has become more settled and complaisant. He is definitely cool and rational.

Conventional? Rigid? He knows the law! The goal Jason is focused on now is his marriage to the young princess, Glauce. He wants to become king of Corinth, and the law—and his future father-in-law, the Old King, who embodies the dominant values of the system—supports him. However devious, there was order in his method. He did what he wanted to do behind Medea's back. Relationship is not so important for him anymore. He doesn't pay much attention to what is going on around him; he doesn't let anything get in his way. Clear about what he wants, he figures out how to get it. Ambitiously and single-mindedly, without consideration for anyone, without consideration for the feelings of his wife, of the well-being of his children—or of his community, he ruthlessly takes the steps he believes he needs to take to pursue his new goal and to achieve it.

On the other hand, Medea, the Asian princess who comes from the edges of the civilized world, who we could say represents the barbarian world, has knowledge of the Earth, of the magical, mysterious, and supernatural. She is passionate, fiery, fierce. Even though her grandfather was Helios, the god of light, the name of her father, Aeëtes, was connected with that of Hades, the god of the underworld.

We know that Medea is the protege and the priestess of Hecate, the goddess of witches and witchcraft. Royal and semi-divine, Medea carries the dark as well as the light. She embodies those things we cannot always control, from normal human emotions to excessive emotionality. She knows those extreme things that reason cannot keep from happening: crimes of the heart, murder, suicide, hurricanes and wildfires. Like clouds building up, getting heavier and heavier, darker and darker, nothing and no one can stop the lightning from striking. Or the thunder that comes after it. There is no stopping this natural force once it tips to the other side.

Near the end of *Medea*, the Chorus says, *"O wretched Jason! / So sure of destiny, and so ignorant!"* Jason, who thinks he's got everything under control, that he's the man in power, is not unlike the mathematicians in Euripides' time who wanted to see the universe in terms of ideas and carefully calculated numerical formulas, and thus ignored the evidence of the physical world around them. In Jason's case, the evidence of the physical world is a very strong and smart and angry wife.

If Jason represents the force of the mind, Medea represents a natural force. The "truth" that Euripides wants to get at in this tragedy is that this natural force which represents the other side of life must be acknowledged and respected. When it becomes difficult and inconvenient, you cannot just ignore it or suppress it, lock it up in the attic of your house or send it out on the road. With his single-minded purposefulness, no matter how hard Jason tries to dominate the situation, however much he tries to manage the way Medea is reacting to him and to his marriage with Princess Glauce—using abusive language and putting words together to distort the reality of things—it doesn't work. During a period when sophistry was praised as a discussion technique, Euripides has Medea say to Jason, *"To me, a wicked man who is also eloquent / Seems the most guilty of them all."*

At the historical moment when the Greek world is on the brink of the Peloponnesian Wars, Euripides is demonstrating that if there is no sincere attempt to reconcile and integrate what Jason and Medea each represent—if there is no balance, no holding of the tension, no polarity or back and forth flow between the conscious and the unconscious, between reason and emotion—if rationality tries to dominate, put the lid on emotions, the odds are that irrational forces are going to burst forth somewhere and erupt to create horror and havoc. In the early 1940s, during World War II, Jung put it this way: "Every extension and intensification of rational consciousness . . . leads us further away from the sources of the symbols and, by its ascendancy, prevents us from understanding them."[19] He also says, ". . . the ever-widening split between conscious and unconscious increases the danger of psychic infection and mass psychosis. With the loss of symbolic ideas, the bridge to the unconscious has broken down. Instinct no longer affords protection against unsound ideas and empty slogans. Rationality without tradition and without a basis in instinct is proof against no absurdity."[20] In Euripides' time, the absurdity was starting a war that lasted for 27 years and destroyed a promising and developing culture. In Euripides' version of the Medea myth, among other things, the absurdity is the murder of innocent children and the future possibilities which they embody. In Greece

---

19   "A Psychological Approach to the Trinity," CW 11, par. 293.
20   "The Structure and Dynamics of the Self," *Aion*, CW 9ii, par. 390, note 79.

it was a time of war. It was the beginning of the end of the Golden Age.

The archetypal human situation of a woman being betrayed and abandoned by her husband could be found on every street in fifth century BC Athens, and can be found on every street where we live today. In his tragedy, *Medea*, Euripides is also saying something else. I really have to emphasize here that I am not talking about "man this" and "woman that." For me, *masculine* and *feminine* represent major principles of life, which, as Jung has so emphatically pointed out to us, are carried by men and women alike, for good and for bad. Euripides' drama shows us what happens when there is no reconciliation or integration of these major principles of life: soul and body, mind and heart, reason and emotion, hate and love, thinking and feeling, technology and nature. He shows us what happens, whether in individuals, communities, or countries, when the major principles of life composed of *masculine and feminine* values get polarized, when there is no vessel of transformation to contain a creative tension of opposites.

Medea and the panoply of feminine values that she embodies and represents cannot be compartmentalized or dominated. She may not be dealt with like a simple object to be controlled, or a nuisance to be analyzed or explained away. In the play, for heaven's sake, Jason is telling Medea that she is not important, and that she didn't really matter all that much to him in the first place. Yes, Jason is telling Medea that she doesn't matter.

The epiphany of truth Euripides is getting at here is that *masculine* and *feminine* principles, conscious and unconscious, the seen and the unseen world, all need to work together in mutual acknowledgement and respect. What Medea embodies is a complex natural force that wants to be recognized and reconciled, integrated with the *other* as one who is equally important and equally valuable.

Watching what happens at the end of Euripides' tragedy can be a shocking and appalling experience for some members of the audience, as this woman who has just mercilessly killed two people, and then her own children, gets away scot-free. She has ruined Jason's life! In the *Poetics*, 75 years after Euripides' death, Aristotle tells us that he was horrified by the events portrayed in this drama. By letting Helios send the *Deus ex machina*, the god in the machine, and by letting her be carried off by the power of the Great Mother, Euripides is exonerating Medea. More than that, on the stage, on the altar of the Earth god Dionysus, the god of life and death, light and dark, he is telling us that the natural force that Medea represents—not only her knowledge and her prestige as a priestess and a shaman, but the legitimacy of her *feelings*—cannot be ignored or suppressed. A woman's hurt and anger, and her suffering, cannot be hidden away and argued or medicated out of existence. The *feminine* in all its complexity may not be ignored with impunity. *Nature* may not be violated with impunity. When Medea is carried off in the chariot of Helios, pulled by two dragons, Euripides is letting the

Sun and the Earth say that Medea and the dark and light values that she embodies exit, and that they live on. Medea represents a very real force in the lives of individual men and women, in the life of communities, and in the life of countries. The point is that she can be dangerous, and that we scorn and insult her at our peril.

THE UNIVERSALITY OF MEDEA'S TRUTH

After examining the play for the story, and giving a psychological interpretation, we have also gotten a sense of the historical background of the playwright. With more awareness of the context in which Euripides was living and of the theater for which he was writing, we have looked for the author's deeper meaning in his own time. Since we regard *Medea* as a classic of dramatic literature, the next question is about the universal and timeless significance of this play. How does its fifth century BC message apply to us in the early decades of the 21st century AD?

I do not want to dwell on my personal apprehensions about current international policies, particularly those of the United States. I'll leave it up to the reader to think about the political situations in many countries around the world today, and what is happening to the global environment. In Euripides' *Medea* we can find a universal significance that has a more profound, timeless, and symbolic meaning than the immediate message of the plot. It is a rather sobering one and can be applied to the period in which we live. For we also live in a time when respect for dialogue and diplomacy, for compromise and respect for *feminine* values—for nature, for natural forces and the unseen world—do not often appear to be serious priorities. To quote Jung again, writing during the Second World War, ". . . the ever-widening split between conscious and unconscious increases the danger of psychic infection and mass psychosis... Instinct no longer affords protection against unsound ideas and empty slogans."[21] His words resonate: "The frightful records of our age are plain for all to see, and they surpass in hideousness everything that any previous age, with its feeble instruments, could have hoped to accomplish."[22]

Three of Euripides' tragedies are closely related thematically: *Medea, Hippolytus*, and *The Bacchae*. In all three the *masculine* denies the *feminine*. As Jung has said, "Rationality without tradition and without a basis in instinct is proof against no absurdity."[23] All three tragedies deal in varying degrees with the shocking consequences of rigidly held ascetic attitudes, the deceptions of sophistry, and naked lust for power. They all deal with anger, revenge, and retaliation—the eruption of violence and the impulse to destroy. In *Hippolytus*, which is a story about the extremes of sexual desire and sexual revulsion, the impersonal, natural

---

21   Ibid.

22   "The Psychology of the Transference," *The Practice of Psychotherapy*, CW 16, par. 388.

23   "The Structure and Dynamics of the Self," CW 9ii, par. 390, note 79.

forces of life are represented by the quarreling goddesses, Aphrodite and Artemis. The irresistible force in *The Bacchae* is embodied by Dionysus himself.

Euripides was more than 70 years old and living in exile in Macedonia, when he wrote *The Bacchae.* Although he never saw it produced, he wrote it to be performed on the altar of Dionysus. The Peloponnesian Wars had been going on for roughly 20 years. They would continue for roughly 10 more, and Athens, physically and economically devastated, and depopulated by plague, would lose her political and cultural leadership in the Mediterranean world.

Briefly and simply, *The Bacchae* is about the retribution of Dionysus against the citizenry of Thebes, who no longer believe that he is the son of Zeus and a god who represents the powerful natural forces of life. Most particularly, Dionysus avenges the attitudes and actions of his cousin, Pentheus, the young king of Thebes, the son of Agaue, who is the sister of Dionysus' mother, Semele. In a terrible scene at the heart of the play, King Pentheus not only publicly denounces Dionysius but he actually physically abuses the god.

At the same time that Pentheus insults Dionysus and denies his divinity and all that he embodies, it is revealed that the young king is a voyeur. The dark, hysterical *shadow* of this rigid, puritanical, controlling young man erupts and carries him away. He only wants to watch, he says, as, deep in the mountain wilderness, the followers of the god, the Bacchae, engage in their secret Dionysian revels to honor the coming of spring. He says he just wants to have a look from high up in a tree, a look at what his lascivious imagination tells him is going to be an obscene and sexually titillating event. As Jung observed, "The more compulsive the one-sidedness, and the more untamed the libido which streams off to one side, the more daemonic it becomes."[24] To teach Pentheus and everyone else in Thebes a lesson, in Euripides' play, Dionysus lets a dreadful thing happen. When the Bacchante become aware that someone has snuck up from behind to spy on them, they break out of their lighthearted, enthusiastic spring dance and get into an utterly extreme animalistic frenzy. Led by Pentheus's own mother, Agaue, in a trance they brutally and bloodily tear the intruder limb from limb.

During his last speech, just before the end of *The Bacchae*, talking about Pentheus, Euripides has Dionysus say, *"This fate he has justly suffered; for no god can see his worship scorned, and hear his name profaned, and not pursue vengeance to the utmost limit; that mortal men may know that the gods are greater than they."* In other words, if the cosmic, impersonal, natural, instinctual, and irrepressible forces of life and nature which are represented by the gods are ignored or violated, there will be retaliation. In *Medea* and *Hippolytus* and especially in *The Bacchae*, directly or

---

24 "The Type Problem in Poetry," *Psychological Types*, CW 6, par. 347.

indirectly, the mother kills the son. To repeat again Jung's words, "Rationality without tradition and without a basis in instinct is proof against no absurdity."[25]

At the end of *The Bacchae*, the Chorus says—and I can imagine the actors standing tall in their masks and flowing robes before the altar of Dionysus, their voices booming out their words to the great audience gathered on the surrounding hillsides—*"If there be any man who derides the unseen world, let him consider the death of Pentheus, and acknowledge the gods."*

Euripides has shown us that Medea, the goddess abused, will rage and retaliate, that the divine *feminine* will have its revenge. His warning was not heeded in his time. Athens went to war for 27 years. In *The Bacchae*, his last and perhaps most powerful play, the author's epiphany of truth is clear. The Earth and the unseen world will have her revenge. The Mother will tear her sons to pieces—the sons who represent the future—and after this dismemberment, there will be no resurrection.

---

25   "The Structure and Dynamics of the Self," CW 9ii, par. 390, note 79.

PART THREE

If there be any man
who derides

the unseen world,
let him consider the
death of Pentheus, and

acknowledge the gods.

—Euripides,
The Bacchae

EDITH

We need to explore other aspects of the Medea myth now, look at it in different ways psychologically, and spend more time on Euripides' characters, Jason and Medea. But first I'd like to return to the analysand, who came to see me after her husband told her she was crazy and should see a psychiatrist.

When Edith realized her marriage partner was having sexual intercourse with a younger woman, someone she was acquainted with, this respectable, highly regarded professional found herself behaving in the "Medea" mode, overwhelmed with homicidal and suicidal emotions, and acting in terrible, violent, and destructive ways. She was afraid she was losing her mind.

Edith was a woman who, you could say, was living her life in the heroic mode. She had a lot of *animus*. Intellectually gifted, a great organizer, very efficient and focused, Edith was an extremely capable and competent person. She had a job to do. Actually, she had several jobs to do. She was a multitalented, multitasking and significantly accomplished woman who always managed to stay on top of things. She had a lot of constructive *masculine* energy.

In her mid-40s, Edith was entering the time of her life when the other side, the unseen and undeveloped aspects of her personality, began clamoring for the opportunity to emerge and unfold. In her case, the wake-up call was not a serious illness or a bad accident—or even a dream about such things—that caught her attention. It was learning of her husband's infidelity.

In order to accomplish her professional goals, Edith had had to be utterly focused and consequent for many years. As Jung has said, though, when we reach noon and the night is born, the unconscious begins to make other demands. Edith had, to use Jung's expression, her name on the door. She was firmly established professionally and socially. In order to achieve this success, however, like more and more women today, she had to neglect certain psychological and emotional aspects of her *feminine psyche*. She was well developed in the giving and doing-for-others sides of the *feminine*. She was, in fact, a very generous person. It was the receiving, containing, and holding aspects of her personality that were less evolved. It was also the part of herself that could be spontaneous and playful, that could be receptive and open to new and different things, that she had ignored.

Growing up, Edith had many advantages and was given many opportunities. However, although she was raised in a family which stressed the importance of intellectual achievement, and rewarded it, she was teased and goaded for her braininess. In other words, she was brought up in a kind of double-bind. The Positive Father voice says to his daughter, yes, you can do it. The Negative Father voice says, No, you just can't get it right, you're only a girl. When Edith found out that her husband was betraying her, the pain of that went right into her old father wound, the *complex* around never being quite good enough. If it was a 90, why wasn't it 100? If it was an "A," why wasn't it an "A+"? Edith came from a generation of women who wanted to have it all, and, given her family background, was particularly determined to be a superwoman. Gradually, though, the demanding negative inner voices were starting to bother her.

However liberated she considered herself to be as a woman, because her husband was a man, his time was always more valuable than hers. After she learned of his unfaithfulness, the vehemence of her anger against him was like a rebellion. From a feeling of despair and desperation, she was also saying: What more do you expect from me? I can't do any more; I can't do any better.

When Edith first came to see me, beyond her profound disappointment and grief, and "Medea rage" at her husband's betrayal and ingratitude, was the realization that she was exhausted and burned out in her profession. Early on, she had this dream: *A woman whose left eye was dislodged by a deep diagonal cut across her bruised head and bashed-in face was brought into a hospital.* Edith was not doing well. However you want to look at it, there were aspects of her personality which were not in good shape—her vision, the way she saw things, her identity.

A lifetime habit of rationalizing and relativizing had effectively put the lid on Edith's true feelings and on the unseen world within her. She had to learn about the symbolic life from scratch. At first it was really hard for her to be in analysis, because she kept worrying about whether she was doing it right. It took her a long time to surrender the aspect of her personality that needed to "do," and which could only give value to herself when she was in action, working either at her job or at home. Being productive! And it took a long time for her to let go of that *negative animus* side of herself, which was highly opinionated, that needed to know and to be right, and always on top of everything. It really took a long time for Edith to be less intensely focused all the time and in her head, and less driven by a sense of duty and of personal responsibility. This was what she seriously needed to do, if she wanted to start to become more whole, let her *Self* naturally unfold, and be deeply connected to her *feminine* soul.

As Jung says so eloquently, "We overlook the essential fact that the social goal is attained only at the cost of the diminution of personality. Many—far too many—aspects of life, which should also have been experienced, lie in the lumber-room among dusty memories; but sometimes, too, they are glowing coals under grey ashes."[1]

Before she could start to respond to the claims of her unlived life and to the untapped possibilities within her, Edith had to slowly peel off those layers of intellectualizing, rationalizing, and relativizing away all kinds of uncomfortable feelings. Her instincts were seriously damaged. She

---

1 "The Stages of Life," *The Structure and Dynamics of the Psyche*, CW 8, par. 772.

was, in fact, in denial about certain doubts and fears she had been having recently regarding her life—questions, qualms. Her attitude was that there were always other people whose lives were much harder. Edith really had to learn that it was safe to have normal human emotions about things that happened to her, without getting lost in out-of-control archetypal emotionality.

Working with me was a different kind of encounter than Edith was accustomed to. I think she experienced me as being subversive. Gradually, she could loosen up, relax and cut herself some slack. I remember the time she proudly told me that, on a recent lunch break, she gave herself permission to stop in at a bookstore, have a cup of coffee, and read an article in a popular magazine. It was quite out of the ordinary for her to do something like that. Those inner voices, that *negative animus* voice, kept telling her, even though she was doing, doing, doing, she was still found wanting. It was a real struggle for Edith to accept that, despite all of her complexity and imperfection, she was in fact quite a remarkable human being.

It is important to emphasize that Edith does not fit the model of the woman in Jung's essay, "The Stages of Life," where he says that second-half-of-life ". . . changes are accompanied by all sorts of catastrophes in marriage for it is not hard to imagine what will happen when the husband discovers his tender feelings and the wife her sharpness of mind."[2]

---

2   Ibid., CW 8, par. 398.

The model Jung gives is certainly not obsolete, but it is not anywhere as pervasive as it was when he wrote the article in the early 1930s. At that time, in the conventional model of a marriage, the husband went out to work in the world and the wife stayed at home taking care of the children. An exception to this was still pretty rare. In Edith's case, and in cases of other women of her generation today, in the second half of life or the beginning of the last third of life, the psychic shift that wants to take place is not necessarily toward the development of unused, more *masculine* aspects of the personality. In these cases, the shift is usually away from one-sidedness, single mindedness, and driven-ness, toward the development and the integration of an authentic and rich femininity.

In Edith we have the model of the woman whose "sharpness of mind" directed the course of her life since she was a child. From the time she went to college and did her graduate and postgraduate work, she had been out in the world and achieving. In Edith's case, we could say she was ready to develop her "tender feelings." It was certainly time for her to free herself from the shackles of patriarchal attitudes and expectations, and to allow herself to think and feel out of her own depths.

Jung says in "The Stages," "Thoroughly unprepared we take the step into the afternoon of life. Worse still we take this step with the false assumptions that our truths and ideals will serve us as hitherto. But we cannot live the afternoon of life according to the program of life's morning . . ."[3]

It was very hard for Edith to make this adjustment, particularly because her idea of the *feminine* was negative. To her, "feminine" meant passivity, dependency, inertia, superficiality, and inferiority. For the same reasons, many men in the second half of life, or the last third, also have to go through quite a struggle to overcome an innately negative picture of the *feminine* within them before they can surrender to the *Self's* urge for wholeness, and achieve a harmonious reconciliation with and integration of *positive anima* values.

Over the years, slowly and gradually, there have been substantial changes in Edith's life. It is as if she were dismembered and put back together again a little differently. She reduced her workload and started to actively explore the significance of the coals still glowing in the ashes of her past. With painful hard work, Edith and her marriage partner were able to reconcile and continue to evolve as a couple, as well as autonomous individuals. In this case, the man and the woman have not gone flying off into different directions. The opposites were actually able to get into a more creative polarity, and integration has definitely taken place on both sides.

---

3   Ibid., par. 784.

JASON

There is no way we can seriously compare Edith with Euripides' Jason. I want to demonstrate that *masculine* and *feminine* principles are not exclusively restricted to gender, and that—with or without the caddishness and callousness—too much one-sided Jason energy in a man or in a woman can stir up the "Medea rage." That is, whether it is something happening between two people, between two different psychological principles in one person, or, as was suggested earlier, between different parts of a community, a country, or the world. Any too much or too little is a negative. When a single-minded, one-sided *masculine* attitude wants to dominate *feminine* values in a man or in a woman, when there is too much Father energy and not enough Mother, too much Logos and not enough Eros, the individual psyche, or the global community, is out of balance and, in some shape or form, there promises to be retaliation—revenge. As Jung has said, the effect of the archetype is always strongest where consciousness is weakest and most restricted, and the greatest danger threatening us comes from the unpredictability of the psyche's reactions.

Euripides' fifth century BC archetypal situation between Jason and Medea gives us a disturbing example of what the backlash can look like when an inferior *masculine* stance of crass opportunism, greed, unrelatedness, lust for power and need for control tries to dominate. We have seen how we can look at Jason's and Medea's behavior on an individual level, as well as on the streets of fifth century BC Athens, and on our streets at home. We can imagine how it looks in our contemporary political world.

As an illustration of a man in a midlife crisis, we can ask ourselves what a hero like Euripides' Jason looks like after he has slain the dragon and gotten his name on the door. In Jung's essay "The Stages of Life," he says the following:

> "The significance of the morning undoubtedly lies in the development of the individual, our entrenchment in the outer world, the propagation of our kind, and the care of our children. This is the obvious purpose of nature. But when this purpose has been attained . . . shall the earning of money, the extension of conquests, and the expansion of life go steadily on . . . Whoever carries over into the afternoon the law of the morning, or the natural aim [that is, biological and social aim], must pay for it with damage to his soul . . ."

Jung goes on to say that the meaning and purpose of the second half of life is culture.[4]

Euripides presents Jason as a man in *regression*. What Jason is trying to do is carry over into the afternoon of life the law of the morning. In spite of the fact that he says, "If

_____
4   Ibid., par. 787.

only children could be got some other way / Without the female sex!," the evidence in the play more than suggests that he wants to stay in the heroic phase and hold on to the biological as well as the social aims of his life. Living quietly in Corinth, after all his exploits and adventures, and after creating a home and having a family, we can imagine that Jason starts to feel restless. We could say he is ignoring the unseen and undeveloped aspects of his psyche, and perhaps living in the past. As Jung puts it in his essay, "Marriage as a Psychological Relationship," what used to be passion, has become duty: ". . . the turnings of the pathway that once brought surprise and discovery become dulled by custom . . . " Jung goes on to say, "This disunity with oneself (between the lived and unlived life) begets discontent, and since one is not conscious of the real state of things one generally projects the reason for it upon one's partner."[5]

As we see in the play, Jason detaches from his wife. He not only forsakes his and Medea's own two sons, but he also rejects being a psychological and emotional father to himself. Becoming submissive, regressive, he aligns himself with his father-in-law, Creon, who is an Old King— and we know from fairy tales that the Old King implies irrelevant attitudes and outworn ideas.

Not really interested in a relationship with a mature woman who is also his peer, Jason wants to go back to

---

5   "Marriage as a Psychological Relationship," *The Development of the Personality*, CW 17, pars. 331a & 331b.

conquering maidens. It appears that he wants to do everything all over again. However, when he remarries, whether
he is aware of it or not, he is no longer a courageous hero
overcoming frightful obstacles; he is a member of established institutions. As Euripides has Medea say to him
sarcastically, *"But you're an aging man, and an Asiatic wife /
Was no longer respectable."* Perhaps a lot more conventional
than he realizes, Jason marries a younger woman who is
still very much in the daughter mode, someone he knows
is going to be compliant and obedient, and not challenge
his male dominance.

In her essay, "The Archetypal Masculine: Its
Manifestation in Myth and Its Significance for Women,"
Barbara Greenfield asks a provocative question. Talking
about Greek mythology, she ponders why we do not have
a picture of men who are simply the peers of women? She
suggests that, "traditionally, men and women have never
been in peer relationships." She goes on to point out that,
except for brothers and sisters, "In most myths . . . men
exist as either tricksters or fathers in relation to women,
and not as soul-mates."[6] The Greek scholar Thomas Cahill
reminds us that, in ancient literature, the only male-female
soul friendship is the one which Homer describes in *The
Iliad* between Hector and Andromache.[7]

6   Barbara Greenfield, 201-202.
7   See Thomas Cahill, *Sailing the Wine Dark Sea*, 34-39.

MEDEA & JASON

We have seen that Medea, in her own time—and we could say in any time—exemplifies quite an extraordinary woman. She came from the East, where the *feminine* principle which she represented was still valued. Once in Greece, however, where a distinctively patriarchal society had emerged and developed, she was not only a foreigner, but she also embodied a threat. In the patriarchal coloring of the myth, much seems to have been made of the fact that Medea abandoned her father, and that this in particular shows what a bad person she is.

Apparently, Jason looked like Apollo. When Medea sees him for the first time, with a little help from Cupid's arrow, she falls deeply in love. Remember that Hera, Jason's patroness and the patroness of the Argonauts, as well as the goddess of marriage, persuaded Aphrodite to persuade Eros to shoot his arrow deep into Medea's heart. Hera wanted Medea to help her protege on his quest of the Golden Fleece. In effect, from the very beginning, the princess of Colchis has the backing of the gods. Medea's exotic golden eyes see the positive *masculine* qualities in Jason. Alas, it is only much later that she experiences and sees his dark side.

Even though Medea was the granddaughter of the sun god, Helios, considering that her father was connected with Hades, and that she was a protege of the goddess Hecate, it is possible to imagine that, from the beginning,

Jason was unconsciously attracted to the dark, dangerous side of this priestess. That is certainly what he is blaming her for at the end of the play, when he is telling Medea that he always knew she was a bad person. In any case, it is probably safe to say that when they met, the chemistry, the hormones, and the *projections* flying back and forth took their breaths away. Between Medea and Jason there was a powerful attraction of opposites on many different levels. It was supported by the goddesses Hera and Aphrodite, and the powerful forces they represent.

When Jason arrived in Colchis, Medea had to make a life-altering decision. She knew that her father, Aeëtes, an Old King, did not want the young Jason and those hearty, virile young Argonauts around. By setting them impossible tasks, he was determined to kill them all. When she goes against her father's wishes, Medea asserts her independence. We need to keep in mind that at this point in the story, Medea is not only a semidivine princess and a priestess, she is a maiden. By disobeying her father and choosing Jason, she opens herself to danger. However, she is also embracing the possibilities of change and of personal development. Being very intelligent, she is not afraid to take a risk.

We need to mention Ariadne here, another divine lady who disobeyed her father and betrayed her brother when she resourcefully and tenderly helped Theseus find his way out of the Labyrinth. After she risked her life and helped Theseus, Ariadne was left behind and abandoned by her

VIOLENCE AND WOMEN

hero. Apparently, according to one version of her story, she was brought back to her father, but in a more popular version she was rescued by Dionysus, who married her.[8]

Medea helped Jason in imaginative ways, using her art to prevent bloodshed. Because of her support, Jason is able to complete his quest for the Golden Fleece without anyone getting hurt. Thinking for herself, relying on her own ability and energy, Medea realizes her personal autonomy. In herself she is a liberated woman. Is it any wonder she has gotten such a bad rap? We have observed that Medea has a strong masculine lineage, light and dark, and that she has the intelligence, will, and presence of a more *masculine* sort. In Euripides' drama, she says to the Chorus, *"Let no one think of me / As humble or weak or passive; let them understand I am of a different kind: dangerous to my enemies / Loyal to my friends."* For this, as we have seen, and because she is a foreigner, she is feared, particularly by those in power and, ultimately, she is renounced as someone who is alien, improper, and evil. Remember her confrontation with King Creon when he casts her out of Corinth.

In the climactic scene of the tragedy, whether Jason recognizes her as such or not, Medea stands up to her husband as a peer and an equal. Clearly, Medea has evolved her own beliefs, values, and code of ethics. She knows who she is. She knows how she feels about things, and does

---

8   Edith Hamilton, *Mythology*, 152.

not acquiescently accept authority imposed on her from outside herself. For this, in Euripides' version of the story, Medea and all that she represents is punished with rejection and banishment. We have seen how, as a principle of life, as goddess abused, with the support of the gods, Medea gets her terrible revenge and brings down *the House of Jason.*

Much has been made of that part of the myth after Jason captures the Golden Fleece, when Medea, in the course of their escape from Colchis, kills her brother Absyrtus. It seems that in the mythologem, there are several variations of what happened. One is that the boy was ambushed and then murdered by Jason in front of Medea. In what appears to be the most prevailing version of the myth, however, Medea, sailing away on the swift Argo with her brother in tow, dismembers Absyrtus and throws the parts of his body into the sea. The father, King Aeëtes, who is in hot pursuit, slows down his ship to gather up the pieces—as Medea knows he will, and the Argonauts get away.

Jung, talking in general about the dismemberment motif, says, "Life is put together again from the broken pieces." Then, between parentheses, he adds a phrase: "(miracle of Medea)."[9] We have to imagine that in the primitive society from which she came, Medea was considered to be a superior person. She was not only a princess and a priestess, but also what we would call a medicine

---

9   "The Dual Mother," *Symbols of Transformation*, CW 5, par. 556.

woman, or a shaman. She was also a goddess, who, like her patroness, Queen Hecate, understood the mysteries of life and death.[10] Dismemberment, transformation, and rebirth are her realm. Knowing that her father, Aeëtes, will stop his ship to gather up the pieces of his son's body, she also knows that her brother will be restored and revivified. She has the magic words!

If we look at Medea's act of dismembering her brother symbolically, it does not have to be seen as cruel or brutal, or unconscionable. As Jung says, dismemberment is part of an initiatory and transformative process.[11] We say things like, "I'm going to pieces," or "I'm falling apart," or "I'm having a meltdown." There's usually an opportunity when these things happen. We have expressions in our language: "So-and-so just tore me limb from limb," or "I'm going to tear you limb from limb," or "Such-and-such is tearing me apart." If we look at the motif of dismemberment psychologically, we might imagine there was a very emotional confrontation between Medea and her brother who, next to her father, is the second man she has to separate from in order to make her deep connection and commitment to her beloved, Jason, and to her own life in the world.

When Medea kills her brother Absyrtus, two distinct but related things are happening. First, she is severing

---

10   Mircea Eliade, *Rites and Symbols of Initiation*, 102.
11   "Transformation Symbolism in the Mass," *Psychology and Religion: West*, CW 11, par. 140.

the bonds of kinship and the possibilities of psychological incest. This brother and sister must be separated now. Second, like a shaman, Medea is guiding her brother towards his own destiny, and fostering his development— hopefully into becoming a more effective human being. Eliade describes dismemberment as a ritual of initiatory death, a preparation for the birth of a new personality.[12] Optimally, a real analysis is about healing, and also about the development of the personality. To quote Jung: "Life is put together again from the broken pieces (miracle of Medea)."

The Argonauts' journey of return from Colchis, the barbarian land in the East, back to civilized Greece in the West, is a chase fraught with dangerous adventures. I'll only mention three.

The first stop they make on the way home is a visit to Medea's relative, Circe, on the island where she lives. Although Circe, who was a sorceress, agrees to perform a ritual of purification over the pair for all their recent deeds, she won't let them stay overnight with her, she says, because Medea separated from their father in such a shocking way. It seems that Circe, who is also a daughter of the sun god Helios, has no tolerance for Medea's dismembering from the family in Colchis. However, in another version of the story, on the journey to Colchis, when Jason and the Argonauts

---

12   Eliade, *Rites and Symbols*, p. 89, 98.

stopped at Circe's island, Jason slept with her. In any case, we can imagine Circe knew her company and didn't want them around any longer than necessary.

The second adventure occurs when the sailors want to spend a night on Corfu, where Medea and Jason have a really close call. It turns out that one of the ships of the Colchian fleet is still right behind the Argo. It is not so easy for a woman to get away from the authority of the Father, outer or inner. In no uncertain terms, the captain of this ship—in the name of King Aeëtes of Colchis—demands of the local king (Alkinoos) that he yield Medea back to him immediately. After some discussion with his wife, the king of Corfu decides that he will return the wayward daughter to her father, only if she is not yet wed to Jason. The sympathetic queen of Corfu (Arete) promptly warns the young couple. Instead of waiting until they are in the home of Jason's parents, which would have been the appropriate thing to do, Medea and Jason have to get married in a hurry.

It is an elaborate and romantic ceremony which takes place late that night in the cave of the divine nymph, Macris (the nymph who was the nurse of Dionysus). The glowing Golden Fleece is spread out on the marriage bed, lighting up the whole grotto. It is quite a celebration. Orpheus is present; there's music and dancing and singing. As the story goes, Hera sends flowers. Hera supports and honors her favorites and, as much as the goddess of marriage loves Jason, she now officially becomes Medea's special protector as well.[13]

The third close call I can't resist mentioning comes when the Argonauts are preparing to stop off in Crete to rest. Medea warns the sailors about the dangerous giant who lives there. When the last of the bronze men, Talos, appears on the sea cliffs ready to throw a huge boulder down on the Argo and crush the ship with all of its inhabitants, Medea gives him a look. Distracted, Talos trips and, as he falls, he grazes his one vulnerable spot—his ankle. He bleeds to death. Thus, the sailors find a safe harbor for the night. I refer to this particular episode in the saga of the return because, as I mentioned earlier, Erich Neumann points out that, whereas originally Medea was considered to be a Goddess of Transformation, in the patriarchally colored version of her myth, she became a wicked witch. I think it is important to note here that Medea did not murder Talos. She just looked at him. In any case, we can imagine that Medea had a look that said, "Don't do that."

There seem to be different versions of what happened when Jason arrived with his new wife in his homeland, Iolcos. The one that appears to have captured the imagination of ancient vase painters involves another incident of dismemberment. To gain back his patrimony, Jason and the Argonauts sailed to the edges of the known world in quest of the Golden Fleece. However, upon his return

---

13   See Kerenyi, *Goddesses*, 36-37.

with Medea, to his great dismay, Jason discovers that his uncle, the Old King, Pelias—the one who had usurped his father Aeson's kingdom in the first place and who, to be rid of him, sent Jason on his death-defying journey—had, during his absence, caused the death of both of his parents. Apparently, he caused Jason's father to kill himself, after which Jason's mother committed suicide. Upon hearing the news of this atrocity, there was no way that Jason was going to turn over the Golden Fleece to Pelias. Medea comes to Jason's aid once again. I wonder if this is where, early in the Medea myth, the motif of revenge and retaliation enters the story, for what she so cunningly did next was what cost her her reputation. Known for her arts of regeneration and rejuvenation, Medea easily persuades the daughters of Pelias to let her make their father young again. First, she demonstrates her skills by chopping up an old ram and cooking it in the cauldron of transformation. A young lamb leaps out of the pot. Then, after being heavily drugged, the Old King Pelias is dismembered by his daughters, and put in the cauldron for renewal. However, this time Medea does not utter the magic words of transformation. Pelias is murdered by his own daughters in a most gruesome way. With Medea's help, Jason is revenged. He flees to Corinth with his helpmate—but without his rightful patrimony.

Except for the killing of the children, which Euripides has Medea do in his tragedy, in the myth it appears that the murder of Pelias is probably considered her most notorious deed. Yet, just as in dreams, when someone dies or is murdered, symbolically it is usually because the aspect of the personality that this figure embodies needs to go, phase out, or, in other words, become depotentiated in the dreamer's psyche. With passion, the Medea *anima* stands up to the Old King and does not let him become an obstacle in their path. The Old King Pelias, and what he represents, has to go.

When Medea uses her art to murder Pelias, what is she in fact doing? Remember that Pelias usurped Jason's patrimony and took over his father Aeson's kingdom. Jason went on his dangerous quest so he could ultimately get it back. We might say that Old King Pelias represents a Negative Father who wants to hold on to his own youth and power, and keep his son from inheriting what is rightfully his. In effect, Pelias is saying to Jason, no matter how hard you try or how well you do, you just can't get it right. You can't have what you want.

When the hero kills the dragon, or the huge serpent—or, in the case of Perseus, the Medusa—and then rescues the maiden from her demon father and terrible mother, we say it is a good thing. Theoretically, *anima* gets separated from Mother, and the hero, or the *masculine ego*, can get on with his life with feeling and relatedness. Perhaps we need to be reminded that, when a woman marries a man, it is she who supports him in becoming a father—a biological or spiritual father—inner or outer or both. Ideally, *masculine* and *feminine* become integrated and something new is created between them. Traditionally, a wife, inner or outer, dream or reality, helps her husband in the development of his masculinity and in the development of his own personal interior as well as exterior fatherliness. Optimally, with his wife's support, a husband has the opportunity to assume his individual and autonomous authority in his own life, in his family, in his field, in the world. But first, the Old King has to die.

We have seen how Jason's Medea/*anima* helped him and guided him through the most difficult parts of his quest. From the first moment Medea was in partnership with him, we can say that, psychologically, Jason had the collaboration of positive unconscious forces. From the instant she saw him, Medea's love for Jason was there to encourage and assist him in his psychological and emotional process of becoming his own man, his own person, and overcoming the fateful dragon. Remember that the Golden Fleece, which represents authority, personal autonomy, and manliness, is guarded by a giant serpent, which Medea sings to sleep. At the end of the journey, Old King Pelias appears as the last obstacle on the path. He embodies the Negative Father who says, You can't do it; you're not good enough; you can't have it. While Medea stands by, his daughters cut Pelias up and toss him into the cauldron of transformation. This time, however, there is no rebirth, no renewal. The magician Medea does not utter the magic words. Rigid outworn ideas and the authoritarian attitudes that this patriarchal Old King represents, to all appearances die with him—possibly giving his daughters the opportunity to one day have their own individual lives.

Leaving Iolcos behind them, Jason and Medea proceed to Corinth, where they settle down and quietly start their married life together, make a home, have a family, and become part of a community. The first half of life!

I think it is important for us to be aware that in the greater story, in the mythologem that Euripides inherited, Jason and Medea are not each asylum-seekers in the same way. Actually, Corinth is the birthright of Medea. Corinth belonged to Medea's grandfather, Helios, who left it to her father, Aeëtes. When Medea and Jason arrive in Corinth, Medea reigns there as queen, and Jason is her co-regent. Euripides, with the poetic license of the dramatist, obviously did not choose to work the myth this way. He changed things in order to use these well-known characters, and the archetypal situation of the man betraying the woman and of the woman getting her revenge, to suit the needs of what he wanted to say. On a deeper level, he was talking about the *masculine* devaluation of the *feminine*, and the repression of the *feminine* principle of life in later fifth century BC Athens and the Greek world in which he lived.

Knowing this about the myth as the playwright found it, doesn't make the attitudes and behavior of Euripides' character, Jason, any less reprehensible—for example, his ingratitude, his disloyalty, greed, and opportunism. However, like a missing piece of a puzzle, it does seem to illuminate still another facet of the plot, and another possible psychological interpretation.

Looking at Jason's story as if it is a dream or a fairy tale, we can say that his Positive Father, Aeson, was displaced by a Negative Father, Pelias. Even though Jason performed all the right, challenging, and heroic feats to achieve his manhood and gain his patrimony, even though he had a loving and supportive wife, and even though he had his name engraved on his door in Corinth, Pelias tells Jason that he still can't have his patrimony. Remember when the Chorus first appears in the play, they say they want to support *"the House of Jason."* It is as if there is still something awry with him emotionally and that perhaps deep down, he is insecure and afraid. We could say Jason inherited division in the Father. This hero seems to be caught between a Father who says, yes, you can do it, and a Father who says, no you can't, much like the experience of my analysand, Edith. Edward F. Edinger considers that the responsibility for Jason's heroic actions "was left in the hands of Medea, as Jason's *anima*. Jason, the *masculine ego*, avoided responsibility, a fatal mistake on the path to individuation, and a suggestion that there was trouble ahead."[14]

---

14   Edward F. Edinger, *The Eternal Drama; The Inner Meaning of Greek Mythology*," 68.

There's another detail in the story that needs to be mentioned here. Jason is also known as *monosandalos*, the man with one shoe. When he makes his first appearance in Iolcos to claim his patrimony from Old King Pelias, with a leopard skin thrown over his shoulders and his long, blond Apollonian hair spilling down his back, he cuts quite a figure. However, there is something wrong with this picture: He is only wearing one sandal. A prophesy had warned Pelias that his usurped kingship would be threatened by the man who arrived on his shores wearing only one shoe. We usually talk about shoes as symbolically representing a standpoint. A man with only one shoe could suggest, for example, an insecure footing, a wavering standpoint, even shiftiness.

By the time we meet him in Euripides' drama, it seems that Jason's long-term psychic and spiritual development are somehow impeded. In his essay, "Marriage as a Psychological Relationship," Jung makes a provocative and paradoxical statement when he suggests that, "Psychological insecurity . . . increases in proportion to social security, unconsciously at first, causing neuroses, then consciously, bringing with it separations, discord, divorces, and other marital disorders."[15] We saw this with my analysand, Edith. We have seen how, while in Corinth, Jason allied himself with the establishment, and eventually in particular with the Old King, Creon, his new father-in-law. We have heard him say that his excuse

---

15 "Marriage as a Psychological Relationship," CW 17, par. 343.

for his marriage to Princess Glauce was that he wanted to gain more wealth and status for himself and his family. With a little imagination and after a glimpse at his history, it certainly appears that, over and above the social security he has with Medea, with their marriage and their family, Jason is after even more concrete outer accoutrements. Is it to cover up a deep inner psychological as well as social insecurity? Is it to compensate for—in spite of everything he did—an abiding Negative Father within, which perhaps he never really stood up to and dealt with sufficiently by himself—as the *dream ego* has to do? If we were looking at this story as if it is a dream…

We describe Euripides' *Medea* as a tragedy. What would be Medea's tragic flaw? By that, we mean a weakness of a basically good person which, under certain unfortunate outer circumstances, comes strongly into relief and causes his or her downfall, or at least an awful lot of trouble. A tragic flaw might also be described as a really bad *complex*, an unhealed wound, or psychological and emotional damage that has never been redeemed and transformed. Remember, Jung says, "…the effect (of the archetype) is always strongest…where consciousness is weakest and most restricted."[16]

Near the end of the play, the Chorus says, *"The fiercest anger of all, the most incurable, is that which rages in the place of dearest love."* Clearly, Euripides' Medea is a woman of

_____

16 "Concerning the Archetypes and the Anima Concept," *The Archetypes and the Collective Unconscious,* CW 9i, par. 137.

extremes. We could say her problem was that she loved too much, and then she flipped and hated too much. Medea gave all for love. When that didn't work out, when she was disillusioned and insulted and humiliated beyond her capacity for endurance, she became violent and homicidal.

It is as if the most negative and destructive aspect of her psyche erupted as a split off, unrelated, driven, and single-minded force against life. We could say that her darkest Hecate-side overwhelmed her personality. We also can't forget that Hera is Medea's protector; to express her anger at Zeus for his infidelities, Hera did cruel things to her rivals. Euripides has Medea say to the Chorus, *"A woman's meek and timid in most matters... But touch her right in marriage, and there's no bloodier spirit."* Not only does Medea's anger erupt against Jason, but also against *"the House of Jason"* and its future, embodied in Jason's sons. That Medea was a woman of extremes *could* be described as her tragic flaw. We also need to remember the passage from Jung which we quoted earlier where he is talking about archetypes: "...the greatest danger threatening us comes from the unpredictability of the psyche's reaction." In Edinger's view, psychologically speaking, a central feature of the Medea myth is the consequence of misusing the *anima*, the man's *feminine* side and soul. He says, "The *anima* was used to advance the aims of the *masculine* ego and not granted respect for her own reality. She turns bitter and is lost to the man."[17]

17   *The Eternal Drama*, 69.

THE POET AND THE WOMEN

Apparently, many of Euripides' female characters are women of extremes. Besides Medea, for example, we have also mentioned Phaedra, who lusted after her young stepson Hippolytus and, upon his fierce and compassionless rejection of her advances, caused his death. We have talked about the brutal murder of Pentheus by his bacchante mother, Agaue.

Earlier we named the tragic dramatists of the fifth century BC: Aeschylus, Sophocles, and Euripides. The famous comic writer of the Golden Age of Greek Theater was Aristophanes, who in 411 BC wrote a play called *Thesmophoriazousae*, meaning "Women Celebrating the Thesmophoria," an annual all-female fertility festival associated with Demeter. In this comedy, which is also known as "The Poet and the Women," the author has the members of the Chorus gang up on a playwright called Euripides for giving women such a bad reputation—something which, of course, in those days the women would never have dared to do in real life on their own behalf. The character named "Euripides" has to make a very quick and dramatic getaway in a winged chariot and, to save his life, he has to promise never to slander women again. Of course, in *Medea*, Euripides' point was that in the late fifth century BC, in the Golden Age, gods and laws and oaths were being violated. He made men—and sometimes gods—look bad. Philip Vellacott, the translator and scholar to whom

I have been referring, thinks the Athenians of the fifth century BC had a bad conscience about women, and that Euripides rubbed salt on the wound. "[The Athenians] knew the standard of morality was low, but they would not have male responsibility for it openly illustrated."[18]

As theater critic and scholar Daniel Mendelsohn says, the Greek playwright's ". . . girls and women—pathetic, suffering, angry, violent, noble, wicked (in other words, all these extreme, difficult women)—were ideal mouthpieces for all the concerns that imperial state ideology with its drive toward centralization, homogenization, and unity necessarily suppressed or smoothed over..."[19] It was acceptable to make fun of these girls and women in a comedy, but they were not to be taken seriously on the stage in a tragedy. Nor was their creator.

Interestingly, Aristophanes' comedy *The Poet and the Women* was written in 411 BC. It was four years later, in 407 BC, shortly after he wrote *The Bacchae*, that Euripides died in exile.

To go back briefly to an interpretation of *Medea* at the personal and individual level, we can say that Medea's tragic flaw is that she was a woman of extremes. We could say she projected her heroic *animus* onto Jason. She loved too much. Then she hated too much. She gave up

18   "Introduction," *Alcestis and other Plays*, 14.
19   See Mendelsohn, "Bad Boy of Athens," *The New York Review of Books*, Feb.13, 2003.

everything, but then she lost everything. That fits, up to a point. Traditionally, though, we say that the tragic character has a downfall. As we have seen, Euripides' *Medea* clearly does not fall. The sun god, Helios, sends her a chariot drawn by two dragons of the Earth. Medea takes off on a magical flight. However heavily laden, in Euripides' tragedy, Medea's flight is an act of transcendence. The gods and the forces of life they stand for are on her side and have been from the beginning. They support her to the end. However much collective patriarchal values of the time reject her, Medea and what she symbolizes and represents will live on. The message is, we spurn her at our peril.

The true tragic flaw in *Medea*, which Euripides brings into relief in his drama, concerns the weakness of a patriarchal system in which the possibilities for a mature peer relationship between a man and a woman are impaired. The tragic flaw in *Medea* has to do with a political organization in which the possibilities between *masculine* and *feminine* principles of life and the potentialities for a creative polarity between the two are broken down. The tragedy of *Medea* is about the failure of a one-sided, single-minded, driven patriarchal attitude which excludes *feminine* values. We can see this in an individual psyche, or in a couple, in a community, a country, or in the world. On the deepest level, this is the archetypal situation that the classical playwright Euripides presents to us in the tragedy of *Medea* for examination and exploration on the inner as well as on the outer stage.

CONCLUDING REMARKS

While I was working on this project, if someone asked me what it was about, and I said that I was exploring Euripides' drama *Medea* from a Jungian perspective, the response to me would invariably be something like, Oh, Medea, the crazy woman who murdered her children. What I have tried to do is present a more differentiated awareness and feeling about Medea, about the *archetype* and the archetypal situation of rage and violence with which she is associated. I hope you will recognize that who she is and what she represents can be understood on many different levels, and that she is much more complicated than "witch," or "child murderer," or "*animus* possessed woman." For Euripides she is a goddess abused. We can see the "Medea rage" in women who sense or believe they are not being valued for themselves, not treated with respect or taken seriously as worthy human beings in their own right, and who, in spite of everything, do have personal feelings, emotional reactions, about what is happening to them. Unhappy women can turn into lethal weapons.

Certainly, in recent decades, in the greater collective in which we live, there have been important and commendable shifts going on regarding the possibilities for women and the possibilities for mature peer relationships between men and women—between *masculine* and *feminine* values, and a creative polarity between the two. I did, however, mention the 28-year-old fellow who told me, quite confidently, that there would always be a double standard. He had a father who taught him to "love them and leave them." But I do see the potential for reconciliation and integration in students and young people I meet. There does appear to be hope for the future in some quarters for more and better individual and personal integration of the opposite principles of life, and for gender equality.

Recently, though, as I was mentally going down a list of women analysands, I realized that most were between their late 40s and mid-70s. Many of them had come with issues having to do with betrayal, rejection, or abandonment at some stage of their lives by present or former partners.

I think we need to consider that even though we see shifts and changes in values, and growing possibilities for a more healthy rapport between the *masculine* and the *feminine*, certainly on the personal and individual level—and that's where it has to start—there are still women we see in our practices who grew up believing that the most important goal in their lives was to be married and loved by a man, and to be mothers. These women have not died out yet. They are still very much around and looking for help, especially as they enter the second half of life, or the last third. These are women who are struggling with their thwarted expectations and disillusionments, and searching for the healing, redemption, and transformation—if that is still possible—of their abiding disappointment and grief, and sense of failure in life. It is not helpful to them to be told by their analysts or therapists or marriage counselors that they shouldn't be angry.

Several times in Euripides' *Medea*, at crucial turning points, Jason makes cracks about women and their sexuality. For example, he says, *". . . you women* (notice he addresses his very individual and semidivine wife as "you women") *. . . you women / have reached a state where, if all's well with your sex life / You've everything you wish for; but when that goes wrong, / At once all that is best and noblest turns to gall."* That is just before he says, *"If only children could be got some other way / Without the female sex!"* And remember, at the very end of the play, in the final confrontation between Medea and Jason, Jason accuses Medea of murdering their children *". . . out of mere sexual jealousy."*

Obviously, Medea was not a product of the Romantic Period in literature and worldview. Yet, we do need to keep in mind that for Euripides, the gods, those forces of life represented by Hecate, by Hera and Aphrodite, and by Eros, supported her passionate sexual relationship with Jason, and his with her.

When a woman is raised in a culture which tells her that she is inferior by herself, that her most serious goal in life is to be married and loved by a man, and if, for her, the love of this man is expressed and experienced through the act of sexual intercourse and in the physical and spiritual resonance around that act, and then discovers that the man she loves has taken this away from her with impunity and given it to someone else, it can be devastating. Such cases still exist and, in some shape or form, there will be the "Medea rage," the desire for retaliation and revenge. There will be bitterness. Biology aside, it is because intercourse for this woman was not sex as adventure or experiment. It was not sex as physical exercise or recreation, or revolution. Or sex commercialized and dissociated from feeling. For this woman, sex was anticipated and experienced as an act of relationship and communication, giving and receiving. An act of love. For such a woman, sexual betrayal can be catastrophic. It was for my analysand, Edith. At that moment of revelation, for her it was like a death.

Just recently, I spoke with a 58-year-old divorced woman who has her own business and who is really doing well. To all appearances, she had made a new life for herself. Nevertheless, as we were talking about these things, she started to cry, and she said to me—and this is more than 12 years after her husband left her for a younger woman—"I feel as if I live in chronic sadness."

While suggesting a more differentiated understanding and feeling around the Medea archetype, I am also implying that for an analyst or therapist, whether male or female, to tell such a woman that she shouldn't be so angry, that men do these things all the time, and that it happens every day on every street in Athens, or anywhere else in the world, is not helpful.

Perhaps a better way for us to deal with this deep emotional and psychological pain when it shows up in the consulting room is to recognize it, receive it, and quietly hold and contain it. Sometimes all we can do for a while is be there, listen, and wait, and, if possible, pay attention to the dreams. When a woman is falling apart in despair, as Jungian analysts we have the opportunity to provide the vessel of transformation, the place for renewal, where the healing of a dismemberment is fostered and where the parts can be put together again. Jung's "miracle of Medea."

To repeat, this suffering is not only about sexual betrayal *per se*. A partner's priorities to having a peer relationship with the woman who is his wife and life's companion can take many forms, including work or play, or family, or addictions. Or emotional absence. The disappointment and thwarted expectations a woman experiences can also be due to physical, verbal, and psychological abuse, as well as later-in-life diseases such as dementia and Alzheimer's, and even death. Disease and death can be experienced as betrayal and abandonment when, bewilderingly, the grief of loss is mixed with anger.

When Susan Smith and then Andrea Yates received their life-term sentences for drowning their children, apparently many women were appalled that they did not receive the death penalty. At the time I was wondering, where is this witch hunt energy coming from? What are these women *projecting* here? As analysts and therapists, we know that women are killing their children all the time, inner as well as outer. We have the evidence in our consulting rooms.

In dreams, we usually look at children as representing new consciousness, fresh possibilities, developing potential for the future. But what about the dreams that come up for so many women during different stages of analysis: miscarriages, abortions, children drowning in bathtubs, in swimming pools, in the ocean; children starving, discovered shriveled up in dresser drawers or as skeletons in closets; ragged, uncared for children found in attics or basements. These are images we can look at as representations of neglected promise, and symptoms of a negative, bitter attitude toward life—of a sense of hopelessness, of passive aggression, or of depression. Underneath these images, we can imagine there might be the anger of a goddess abused.

Mothers wound their children all the time, especially when they take out their unhappiness, frustration, and disappointment in their husbands and their marriages on them. What about the women in our consulting rooms, including the aging daughters of dissatisfied and unfulfilled mothers, who are poisoned by their mother's bitterness, suffocated by their mother's neediness, possessed by their insecurity, impaled by their envy, frozen by their coldness, withered by their emptiness. These children, these daughters (and sons) of unhappy women, of internalized Negative Mothers, are often the victims of the "Medea rage."

What can be more lethal to herself and others than an unhappy woman, than a wife and mother whose expectations in life and for life have been thwarted, denied, or crippled? See the witches in our fairy tales! As Edinger puts it, "The *anima* was used to advance the aims of the *masculine ego* and not granted respect for her own reality. She turns bitter and is lost to the man."

As I have suggested, disappointment, broken promises, thwarted expectations, insult and humiliation, the feeling of being trapped and stuck, and on top of all that alienation and exile, poverty, dependency, and the loss of personal dignity and opportunity—these are elements that can combine to incite in a woman anger, violence, and the impulse to destroy. She can act it out, or turn it against herself. There are many different ways a woman who feels betrayed, rejected and abandoned can destroy her future—her own as well as the future of her children.

,

EPILOGUE

In the West, we are heirs to the ancient tragic split between *masculine* and *feminine* principles. As Jung reminds us, this polarization of opposites endangers not only the fate of individuals, but—especially with the threat of authoritarian *masculine* attitudes towards power looming again in our history—it also presages the political fate of our nations, and the destiny of our planet.

Consider this: For the individual person, the greater collective, and the Earth to survive and thrive in the future, it is crucial that, as men and women, we recognize, honor, and integrate positive *feminine* values, not only in our personal lives—where we need to start—but also in the world around us.

Euripides vividly demonstrates that *Medea*, as woman and as goddess abused, embodies an archetypal force of Nature. She lives. She will find ways to get her revenge.

BIBLIOGRAPHY

Cahill, Thomas. *Sailing the Wine Dark Sea: Why the Greeks Matter.* New York: Doubleday, 2003.

Edinger, Edward F. *The Eternal Drama: The Inner Meaning of Greek Mythology.* Boston & London: Shambala Publications, 1994.

Eliade, Mircea. *Rites and Symbols of Initiation: The Mysteries of Birth and Rebirth.* Trans. Willard R. Trask. New York: Harper & Row, 1958.

Euripides. *Alcestis and Other Plays.* Trans. Philip Vellacott. Middlesex, England: Penguin Books, 1965.

----------- *The Bacchae and Other Plays.* Trans. Philip Vellacott. Middlesex, England: Penguin Books, 1965.

----------- *Medea and Other Plays.* Trans. Philip Vellacott. Middlesex, England: Penguin Books, 1968.

Greenfield, Barbara. "The Archetypal Masculine: Its Manifestation in Myth and Its Significance for Women," in *The Father: Contemporary Jungian Perspectives,* ed., Andrew Samuels. London: Free Association Books, 1985.

Hamilton, Edith. *Mythology: Timeless Tales of Gods and Heroes.* New York: Mentor Books, 1942.

Harper Collins. *Atlas of World History.* Ann Arbor, Michigan: Borders Press, 1989.

Hartnoll, Phyllis. *A Concise History of the Theatre.* London: Thames and Hudson, 1976.

Jung, C.G. *The Collected Works.* (Bollingen Series XX). 20 vols. Trans. R.F.C. Hull. New Jersey: Princeton University Press, 1953-1979.

Kerenyi, Carl. *The Gods of the Greeks.* Trans. Norman Cameron. Middlesex, England: Penguin Books, 1958.

----------- *Goddesses of Sun and Moon*. Trans. Murray Stein. Dallas, Texas: Spring Publications, 1979.

----------- *The Heroes of the Greeks*. Trans. H.J. Rose. London: Thames and Hudson, 1981.

Kitto, H.D.F. *Greek Tragedy*. London: Methuen and Co., 1966.

Leonard, Linda Schierse. *Meeting the Madwoman*. New York: Bantam Books, 1993.

Macgowan, Kenneth & Melnitz, William. *Golden Ages of the Theater*. Englewood Cliffs, N.J.: Prentice-Hall, 1959.

McNally, Terrence. *The Master Class*, New York: Dramatists Play Service, 1996.

Mendelsohn, Daniel. "The Bad Boy of Athens." In *The New York Review of Books*, February 13, 2003.

Nafisi, Azar. *Reading Lolita in Tehran: A Memoir in Books*. New York: Random House, 2003.

Neumann, Erich. *The Great Mother: An Analysis of the Archetype* (Bollingen Series XLVII). Trans. Ralph Manheim. New Jersey: Princeton University Press, 1974.

----------- *The Origins and History of Consciousness* (Bollingen Series XLII). Trans. R.F.C. Hull. New Jersey: Princeton University Press, 1973.

Random House College Dictionary: Revised Edition, 1975.

Roberts, J.M. *The Hutchinson History of the World*. London: Hutchinson & Co., 1976.

Walker, Barbara G. *The Woman's Encyclopedia of Myths and Secrets*. San Francisco: Harper & Row, 1983.

www.ingramcontent.com/pod-product-compliance
Lightning Source LLC
Chambersburg PA
CBHW020706270326
41928CB00005B/294